A Simple Life

A Story of Sid Oakley

A Simple Life

A Story of Sid Oakley

Kathy Norcross Watts

Winterberry Books

Winston-Salem, North Carolina

Cover design and back cover photographs by Claire Ashby: Sid Oakley crystalline pot 2001; Sid Oakley pastel, 2003.

Front cover photograph by Kathy Norcross Watts.

Winterberry Books

4440 Winterberry Ridge Court

Winston-Salem, NC 27103

(919) 691-4451

winterberrybooks@bellsouth.net

ISBN: 978-0-6151-4476-4

Acknowledgments

Thank you to all those who have in some way moved me forward in this writing of a book: to Pat, Lisa, David and Hallie Oakley for sharing Sid with me during his last year and for sharing memories of him with me afterwards; to those of you who told me your favorite Sid stories; to Nellye Tunstall and Mary Lindsey for teaching me about old times; to Paul Mihas who read many less appealing versions of my work and instead of telling me to stop encouraged me to write in ways I'd never tried; to Jaki Shelton Green who told me I could do that which I did not believe I could; to Pat Oakley, Laura Santos, Brad Tucker, Lou Proctor and Bette Laursen for proofing my work; to many editors who've published my other writing: Mark Schultz, Thad Ogburn, Suzanne Brown, Adrienne Johnson Martin, Dan Holly, James Edwards and Harry Coleman; to Chuck Adams, who did not publish my writing, but instead of saying "no" asked me a question; and to David Perry who did say "no" but encouraged me still.; to Lynn Ennis who gave me a place to put my extra material with which I could not bear to part.; to Mary and Chuck Munn who loaned me their guest room in Wrightsville Beach so that I would have place of peace in which to write—and who always provided a full coffeepot; to Bette Laursen and Allison Parrott who watched my four children and gave me time to write; to the Triangle Community Foundation which awarded me a grant at a critical time in my work.; to the N.C. Humanities Council which awarded me the Linda Flowers Award for a part of this story; to my parents who provided me the education and created the drive in me that compels me to write; to Hoover for finding Mildred; and to her husband Bill for sharing his wife with me.

To the memory of Sid and Mildred

for reminding me that every single person matters.

To Hoover and PeeWee and Mary Catherine

for teaching me about faith.

To Jack, Michael, Daniel and Kate

for showing me my blessings each day.

And to Dudley

for telling me I could do this, for giving me time away to do it,

and for never doubting for a moment that I would.

Sixteen Pots

Written by Robert "Harmonica Bob" Waldrop for Sid Oakley in 2000
to the tune of "Sixteen Tons" by Merle Travis, 1949.

Some people say Sid is made out of mud
Sid he's made out of muscle and blood
Muscle and blood and skin and bone
A mind not weak and a back that's strong

> He threw sixteen pots
> An' what'd he get
> Another day older and he's deeper in slip
> Saint Peter don't you call him cause he cain't go
> He owes his soul to the pottery store

Clay saw Sid comin' but didn't move aside
Some pots got thrown, an' some got fired
One hand of iron and one hand of steel
If the right one don't throw it then the left one will

> Chorus

Well he was born on mornin' when the sun didn't shine
Picked up his shovel, walked to the clay mine
He threw sixteen pots while the kiln was cold
Pat said well now bless my soul

> Chorus

He was born one mornin' in a drizzlin' rain
Glazin' and throwin' are his middle names
He dug clay from a canebrake and ground it up fine
Well Pat she made him walk the line

> Chorus .

Reprinted with permission from Robert "Harmonica Bob" Waldrop, 2006.

Prologue

Something so simple as maypops strangling my yellow rose takes me straight back to the last summer I spent with Sid Oakley.

"Don't weed those," I tell my husband, convinced as I am that the odd-shaped leaves portend the purple-pink bloom.

I can see him still, dressed in some soft-worn shirt, his white socks clearly visible, his dark horn-rimmed glasses framing crinkled eyes. I think this weed is a sign from Sid, and I'm determined to stop my husband from removing the vines. He pulled them before, a year after Sid died, and I've felt their absence ever since. Sid's absence.

I miss him still. After he died, I'd hear snippets of "Time to say goodbye" from Romanza on National Public Television's used car campaign, and I just knew he was sending me a sign. He'd played the song at his funeral, which he'd orchestrated himself. I'd been filling my goats' water buckets, pushing aside an inconvenient weed, when I realized that the white-fruited green orb on the vine climbing my wild rose was the maypop he'd told me of. I'd kept his secret sign to myself, and that's when my husband whacked it with our weed eater.

For me, Sid was bigger than life. I know now that I believed whatever he told me and that I trusted him implicitly. For me, that's unusual, and it's also why it's important to keep in mind that I'm not an objective journalist when I write of my friend Sid. I've struggled with whether to tell the story of how he became the man he did, or whether to simply share his philosophy in his own words. In the end, though, I must share the final story he told me. For to me, it shows better than anything else the kind of man that he was. His story shows that every single person matters.

So be prepared: Sometimes I'll write like a reporter, sometimes I won't. I'll cross the boundaries of objectivity and forget that I ought to remain on one side. I'll become so entrenched in the story he sent me to find that I might forget the focus of this project, which for the first two years I thought would be Sid. I'd thought it would be easier to write a biography since I'd be able to avoid creating dialogue, a challenge which terrified me. I couldn't have been more wrong.

I suppose I also need to confess to my lack of expertise in both pottery and painting. In the early months, I thought I'd learn enough about those topics to comment on Sid's work, but again, I was wrong. I finally decided to write about the little bit he told me in the way he told me, for that is my expertise.

Looking back, I'm embarrassed at just how gullible I was. As a reporter, I'd been taught to question, yet still I eagerly documented each word that Sid said, for I loved to hear him talk. I've reviewed old newspaper stories only to see that I was not the first reporter to write half truths and attribute them to Sid. Those yellowed pages provide me some comfort now. To this day, I know not whether the mistake came first, and Sid simply accepted it, or if he actually helped reporters to make leaps in their logic that they shouldn't have.

Oh, I tried to balance my view of him. I talked with many, many people who knew him. What struck me during those talks is that each knew him in a special way, and some became right defensive of those memories when I shared other conversations I'd had. Not everyone had come to see the many facets of this complicated man. Sid was not simple, nor was his life, but he made it seem so.

I also need to admit that I know he lied to me. Or rather, he withheld the truth from me. He never told me he was dying. I may have sensed it, but I couldn't acknowledge it. From the first time I met him, I'd felt an urgency to talk to him and write, as if my time were running out. But he never told me that he would leave so soon, and it's taken me a while to forgive him for that.

Yet even knowing what I know now: that I wrote some of the same exaggerations that other reporters wrote, that the encouragement he gave to me he'd given to others many times before, that he may have used me in his attempt to obtain publicity for his store and that in my naïveté I felt honored, even knowing all this, I know that Sid Oakley was a great man.

And I know that not only did he give me the gift of a morning every week or two for the last year of his life, he also gave me a story that would change my life. Looking back, I see that he knew it then. But it's taken me time to fully understand the power of what he told me, of what he showed me. To realize that I was meant to spend those mornings with Sid, but that what I thought I was meant to write may not have been the reason I met Sid after all.

Chapter 1

He never smoked when we talked. He didn't even smell like smoke. But the thread of tobacco smoke lingers through his story, from his beginning as the second son in a sharecropper family on a tobacco farm outside of Stem to likely what will cause its end.

Sid Oakley sits in front of a massive brick fireplace at Cedar Creek Gallery, the pottery and fine craft gallery that he began with his wife Pat in 1968.

The gallery's somewhat hidden in an overgrown farm-turned-forest off Falls Lake and holds work from more than 200 craftspeople from across the country. It forms an eclectic paradise outside the rural southern town of Creedmoor. Years ago, the town boasted a larger tobacco market than Durham. It was known as "Mule Town," due to prodigious mule sales made possible by its location on the Southern Railroad line. Now the small town of about 2,500 serves as a bedroom community for Raleigh, just a quick 20 minutes down NC 50.

A customer must know where to look for Cedar Creek Gallery. It's not a place a person might pass on a highway, though it sits within two miles of Interstate 85. It's wedged in the woods, its buildings nearly camouflaged by pines and perennials. A neighbor down the road was arrested for making moonshine a few years back after sheriff's deputies found a cache hidden in the dog house. Another neighbor fills his yard with painted wooden cutouts that vary according to holiday. This is still country life outside small-town North Carolina.

It's so quiet that the crunching of the gravel drive is amplified amidst the bluebird's song. Old tobacco barns surround the cypress-sided gallery. Today, beauty berries are blooming, but at Cedar Creek something is always blooming. Clay statues of personable old jewel-bedazzled buzzards hide amid the Turk's cap hibiscus, whispering like the old ladies Sid modeled when he heard them nitpicking at an art opening in the 1970's.

A middle-aged pudgy black lab sits at the front door beneath a sign that cautions, "Please don't feed the dog—Jeremiah is on a diet." The first room is filled with pots, all sorts of pots and bowls and platters and plates and even lamps made from pots. Displays include traditional functional stoneware in earthen tones as well as brilliant crystalline ceramic base lamps in turquoise and Chinese red. Soap colored amethyst and cobalt and rainbows of candles fill in nooks and crannies on the shelves. Glass ornaments dangle from the ceiling above jewelry cases filled with hand-blown beaded necklaces and earrings and carved gold and silver rings. There are handcrafted wooden toys and tables, baskets and woven rugs. The gallery hugs an atrium filled with a bamboo garden.

A layer of dust covers Sid's studio, and a painting he's begun hangs on an easel. Above the windows, he's taped a series of Matisse quotes that reflect on art and on life, the proclamations yellowed over time.

Sid resembles a gangly, too skinny scarecrow. He looks a little awkward in his frame, an inch of his white cotton crew socks peeking from beneath the hem of his faded blue jeans. He sits in his rocker before the fireplace, stretches his arms behind his neck then settles down to talk. He seems genuinely surprised by what he's accomplished during his 70 years.

His hands look an unlikely pair to have painted the vibrant flowers with the sensitivity that his canvases capture. His knuckles bulge, and perhaps even ache. Some speculate that's why he's painting more now. But he doesn't talk about that. He talks about the new glass studio his daughter is building. He's acting as contractor, sorting out zoning issues and debating the size of the bathroom.

Sid's writing a play now, too. "I've had Emma deliberately forgetting," he jokes, "and maybe it's affecting me, too."

He's just completed another project. He wants to talk about the newly chinked Effie Sherron tobacco barn he moved back to the Cedar Creek land. Its interlocking logs have been sealed with cement and a big old rock acts as a step into what will be extra storage space for the gallery. We walk out to the barn, and it still smells smoky sweet. Sid thinks it makes sense to save the old building, strengthen it and give it a new purpose.

"There's Brad Tucker's studio," Sid points out. "When Pat and I first met Brad, we liked Brad, we didn't like his pots."

He tells me that Tucker's been here 20 years, sharing a passion for simple, functional pots, developing his own following of people who flock to his kiln openings at his studio near the pond.

In his shop Sid has posted an old newspaper article that quotes him proclaiming: "There is no way you'll ever catch me making fine porcelain," yet that is what he's best known for now. The faded paper seems to be a visible sign that he's not afraid to contradict himself.

Sid lives by a simple philosophy: "Pursue what you really love to do." He truly believes his mantra. "Money or at least enough to live on will be a by-product. You miss out too much on what's real important when you concentrate on making money."

It's a lesson he's passed on to his children, to other potters, to other artists and to just about anyone else who stops by the gallery to talk for a while.

Perhaps the message sounds unusual coming from Sid, who says he started out with "absolutely nothing." For many people, the risk of doing what they love oftentimes is overcome by practicality. For Sid, however, it seems the question has never been "Could he?" but "How could he?"

Over the years, he's accumulated a host of honors. In 1981, he was commissioned to make a series of pots for the Smithsonian Institution's catalog. In 1983, he was named a Distinguished Alumnus of Campbell University. In 1989, UNC-Wilmington recognized him as a N.C. Living Treasure. His work is included in collections at the North Carolina Governor's mansion, the N.C. Museum of History, the Duke University Art Museum, the Chrysler Museum and the Folk Art Museum in Tokyo.

Potters from all over the country cite his influence. He's best known for his crystalline glazes on Asian-influenced forms. But many craftsmen know Sid in another role: He was their teacher, their mentor. He provided them guidance, as well as space and equipment to hone their skills, and he sold their work once it reached his standards.

More importantly, though, people from all walks of life talk of his ability to encourage people to follow their own creative paths. They call him "a giver," "an iconoclast," "a Renaissance man."

When I met him, I had expected to be intimidated.

Instead I found a man who looked like he could be my grandpa, who talked with the enthusiasm of a graduating high school senior, who had the wisdom of a prophet. His life experiences resemble a patchwork quilt, where swatches of unexpected colors and patterns that would clash on furniture in a sitting room come together to form a cozy cover unique to him.

I knew I wanted to write his story. I didn't know that I would fall in love with this old potter, with his passion for creativity, with his gift for encouragement. I didn't know that I would feel called to fulfill his last great "idear." Even then, though, I felt we must've been meant to find each other.

We're drinking coffee today, as we will each time we talk. He takes his black.

"Sid, I'm really not supposed to take anything from people I write about," I tell him. He had sent home an ice blue crystalline pot with my husband to thank me for a feature story I'd written about the gallery. I fear it's a conflict of interest, but I can't force myself to give it back.

"Oh, he gives away pots all the time," Manager Patrick Hurley chimes in from the counter. I think he's just saying that to make me feel better.

Sid sets down his coffee mug, cups his hands around it for warmth and leans forward across the wooden table. He boasts of the 800 pencils he bought on E-bay for $10, and he gives me 20 sheets of stickers he bought on-line for my children. He's already mailed a selection to his grandchildren.

"Lucas and Sydney loved them," he says. He simply can't resist a good deal, can't escape the memories of eating fried sweet potatoes and boiled chicory roots for breakfast during the Depression, of pulling a sack of turnip salad each morning to carry to Stem School as payment for a hot lunch there.

"I always thought everyone else was poor," he says in all seriousness. "I didn't know any different."

He simply doesn't see his path through life as unique. He worked hard. Everyone did back then. What was unusual, he admits, is that he graduated from college and then obtained a master's degree. It wasn't until he was in his mid-30's that he chose to pursue his pottery and painting full time.

He succeeded. To hear him talk, it seems like no big deal.

Chapter 2

When first we begin meeting, Sid seems a little self-conscious at the attention. He claims, "I don't think there's enough to write about me." I argue with him and recount the value I see in the lessons he's lived: that if someone works hard he can succeed, that it's important to enjoy your life's work, that it's important to encourage others. That's the story, I tell him again and again, as if he cannot see the purpose of his own life.

"I've been thinking about this," Sid says. "I really think you're making a mountain out of a mole hill."

He steers the conversation away from himself and instead, starts telling me the story of a little girl from his childhood who had been sent home from school because she was black.

It has been nearly 60 years, and still he seems bothered by a bus ride he took to Stem School back around 1945. The memory's so clear for him, it's evident he's been thinking about it a lot lately.

He was 12 years old, and it was Mildred's first day at school. Sid remembered she wore a yellow dress, her hair in pigtails. She was a petite child, so tiny that her feet didn't touch the floor when she sat down in her chair. Her family lived nearby; in fact they were Sid's distant relatives. Her parents had three other children, and several years later, Mildred was born.

She was black. Her parents were white.

"They accepted Mildred into their family, even the husband did," he says. "Nobody in the community really objected to it. She was accepted. At least the poor people did.

"When the time came for her to go to school, I was on the bus that morning. She was excited and had a smile on her face. Then when she got into school, they wouldn't let her go into the classroom. They made her sit in the hall.

"I remember talking to her in the hallway there because I knew her. She didn't really know what the problem was. The police came and took her away. I don't know if they carried her back home, and then carried her to some black family in Stovall, who maybe adopted her. But you can't find out anything about it now."

He has both my attention and my curiosity.

"That night after they took the girl away from school, three yokels from Stem got halfway drunk and went to their house and demanded that the man, the father of this girl, be turned over to them. The woman's husband met them on the porch with his gun and told them if they didn't get the hell away, he wouldn't hesitate to shoot them, and to never come back.

"Obviously she had some kind of affair with somebody, but the husband still stayed there and defended her."

He's tried to find the little girl, but no one wants to remember what the community recalls as a shameful event. Sid agrees that it was shameful, but for him the shame is in how the community treated a seven-year-old child, and not about how a black child came to be born into a white family.

Sid has never forgotten his image of Mildred.

"I thought about calling Oprah to see if she could find her. She would have the resources. I just cannot fathom someone growing up being loved, then being sent away.

"That's what you need to write about," he tells me. "Find Mildred."

For years, I'd passed the unobtrusive brown and tan sign on NC Highway 50 that stated "Pottery and Fine Crafts," but, to be honest, the sign didn't draw me there. My husband knew I was always looking for story ideas, and he had met Sid, who was at that time battling the county government for a rezoning for his daughter's studio. The commissioners directed my husband to "find a way to help him work this out." He knew that meant Sid was important.

"I think he taught pottery to alcoholics or something," my husband said.

So I set up an interview, met with Sid and his wife Pat for about two hours, and wrote a feature story that I thought was new to the world and later learned was just one more marketing ploy that Sid had adeptly seized. In the years since I first met him, I've found dozens and dozens of stories about his gallery, and each writer told similar stories with similar enthusiasm. I began at the beginning. I walked with him into a smoky old tobacco barn that he had moved back to Cedar Creek. I wrote that he had a double major—his wife says he did not—I wrote that people need to "do what they love to do and the money will come." Sid's creed.

Sid had sent me the pot with his thank-you letter, and inside the pot I had found a photocopied newspaper story about the Korean President receiving one of Sid's pots during his visit to the United States.

It wasn't so much his apparent fame that had sparked my idea to write his biography. It was talking with Sid and hearing his "poor boy done good" story. I had written to Sid, he had agreed, and I was now driving home from our first manuscript meeting with a mandate from him that I wasn't sure I could fulfill.

I'm not a detective, after all, and I know the white mother is dead. I have four children, all of whom are younger than 10 years old. And I live on a farm with goats, chickens, donkeys, dogs, cats, a guinea pig, a hamster and a horse named Magic. I don't particularly want to go around spreading rumors about an affair that had happened 60 years ago. I don't know who to ask, what to ask or how to ask it. Tactfully. I cannot figure out how to find her without saying why I am looking for her.

So I plan to continue writing newspaper stories in snatches of time between life's regularities, and I decide to avoid Sid and Cedar Creek for a couple of months. But when I walk in Wal-Mart or buy groceries at Food Lion, I begin watching and looking into the faces of every old black woman I see wondering, "Could you be Mildred?" I know she is pretty. And she is light-skinned. And she must be about 60 by now. So I look for pretty light-skinned 60-year-old black women, and I see there are many, many women who meet that description. I consider how improper or strange it might be to ask, "Are you named Mildred?" or "Do you know anyone named Mildred?" I study old black men, too, wondering, "Could you be her father?"

In her white mother's mind, something must have set him apart from the rest of her world, for her to take the risk that she did. I look for really old black men with broad shoulders, warm smiles, intelligent eyes with a hint of pain, proud but not arrogant, confident but not angry. I see many, many men who fit my imagined description of Mildred's father.

On rare occasions, I ask my question, "Do you know anything about an adoption of a little black girl that happened 60 years ago because she was sent home from the white Stem School?" Or something to that effect. People refer me to others they know who might know someone who might know what happened. I call and follow up on several leads. I try never to explain my question in detail on the phone.

I really don't have time to find this child, now a woman, for Sid, and even if I did have time, I really don't know how to find her. He doesn't know her last name, and it's clearly a topic that no one wants to talk about.

I decide I'll keep talking with Sid to gather his history for my book. I'll make an occasional effort to find Mildred, once I figure out how to ask about her without spreading rumors.

Chapter 3

He had me from the first time I met him. He hinted at his poor beginnings, seemed modest about his accomplishments, and I immediately thought, "Everyone could learn from his story." It took me months to recognize what a masterful storyteller he was. Perhaps, though, that's why I felt drawn to him. I'd grown up perched on a stool listening to my Grandma Selma tell me stories while she shucked corn and snapped string beans in her Greensboro kitchen. She'd tell me the same stories over and over again, yet I longed to hear her tales.

Truth be told, I'd avoided him for about three months, but in December I'd once again felt a strong need to talk with Sid, so I'd called him again, and we'd scheduled a morning meeting.

It's early January, cloudy and cold. We sit in Sid's fluorescent-lit office for our second meeting. He's stacked papers and books in precarious piles on the desk, and a fine layer of dust covers everything. I balance the tape recorder on the pile nearest Sid. I'm not sure how to work the inexpensive machine since in regular interviews I never use one, but I figured his words needed to be recorded.

"Here, take half these apples," Sid says. He pushes a paper bag across the desk toward me. "No, take more than that. Burnice brought these to me, and they are the best apples."

I add a few more then set my sack aside. Today, he seems to have almost outlined what he wants me to know and to write. He was born November 6, 1932 to Jeanette Jackson Oakley and Earlie Oakley on what was known as the Patty Daniels Farm. The land sat near crossroads in the county called Shoofly and Providence and Tally Ho, and was far enough northeast to be out of reach of Camp Butner, a 40,000-acre training camp that the U.S. Department of Defense built in 1942 to train troops during World War II. The camp stretched over portions of Granville, Person and Durham counties, and nearly 400 families, mostly in lower Granville County, had moved to make way for troops, tanks and artillery.

At one time, Camp Butner, as it came to be known, housed 40,000 troops and a $6 million hospital for wounded soldiers as well as a stockade for prisoners of war. Construction of the camp closed five black schools in the area. For people living during the Depression, a project by the Department of Defense would have meant jobs, but the people there fought the development of their land for the training camp. Much of the land had belonged to the same families for years.

Sid's family lived across a field from his Grandmother Addie's house in the countryside outside of Stem, a town about four miles away. Sid's father was a tobacco sharecropper on his mother-in-law's farm, and the family's livelihood revolved around the cycle of tobacco. He had two brothers, Sam and Pete, and a sister, Hallie. The family lived in a one-room log building with a lean-to for a kitchen. Their home was small, but always neat and clean. It was the midst of the Depression, and though neighbors didn't have much, they shared what they could, even if it was only a tomato from the garden when they went visiting.

As a child, Sid seemed different, more sensitive, perhaps, than many children, especially boys his age. Though hog killing was a regular part of life, "I would close my eyes and look the other way," Sid admits. He preferred yard work and growing flowers to shooting guns. He enjoyed movies and drama. He liked making things with his hands and reading. He remembers details and colors: his mother's black friend who wedged a pinch of red dirt between her cheek and gum like snuff, the white dirt hole filled with kaolin clay that everybody in the community used to whitewash the inside of their fireplaces.

Sid remembers the 12-mile wagon trip to Oxford that his mother made to purchase the few items the family didn't make itself. They traded corn for wheat flour and ground it at Gooch's Mill, an old grist mill in Stem. His Uncle Henry cooked sugar cane in a big vat over a hot fire, and neighbors came to share. He recalls his first battery-operated radio and in later years, it was he who took the papers requesting electricity around for his relatives to sign. He had a vested interest in the new technology since one of his chores was to clean the oil lamps.

On Fridays, the ice man and the fish man would stop by the Oakley house.

"It was such an incredible joy," Sid smiles. "You knew you were going to have an incredible supper and sweet iced tea."

On Saturdays, Sid and Hallie spent a dime each to go to the Carolina Theater in Oxford. Later they'd argue about who was prettier: Betty Grable, Sid's favorite, or Shirley Temple, Hallie's choice. I can see Sid sitting with his great-grandmother, Susan Ross Moss, who would come by the house and spend several days at a time telling him stories, confiding to Sid how cute she thought the Yankees were when she was an 18-year-old girl.

"I suspect she was pretty close to one." Sid has a twinkle in his eye. She told him that her great-great-aunt was Betsy Ross.

Each year, Sid and his buddies looked forward to the county fair, which at that time brought with it "the hoochie coochie show."

"It was very, very authentic," Sid remembered. "For months we talked about it." I don't ask for any more details, though I get the feeling he would have told me.

He'd help his mother around the house, picking vegetables or peeling potatoes, whatever she needed. Supporting his mother was his job. Whether he knew it then or not, he sensed the tension in his home, friction that arose because his father drank too much and his grandmother bickered with his mother.

"My father was an alcoholic," Sid says. "Many times I wished that he would die. Then, when he died, I thought God was going to strike me dead. I just really, really felt guilty about that, but I had seen him drink up so much."

I can picture the tight bun stretching his Grandmother Addie's face sharp, the chocolate drops hidden in her home that he had to earn by carrying in firewood, the pellet gun propped in the corner that he would have never dared to touch, the Sunday dinners at her home where his family wasn't included.

When Sid's father died in 1945, he left his sons the tobacco business. Sid hated it. Four days a week, the brothers would wake up at 5 a.m. and go to work, taking out a barn of 500 sticks of tobacco and unloading it at the pack house before breakfast, soaked with dew before 10 a.m.

Like many tobacco farmers, Earlie Oakley borrowed money to grow his crop. When he sold the tobacco, people would come by to collect their payments. A few months after his father died, a man from Stem drove up in front of their house in a gleaming black car to collect his payment. Sid's mother met him in the yard and told him when the crops came in, she'd pay. He looked beyond Sid's mother and saw the pack house, ambled to its steps and peered inside at the hams and side meat curing from the rafters. He said he'd take the meat as payment.

His mother bristled up like a mad mother hen when somebody bothers her biddies.

"I've never seen anybody get so furious," Sid says. "She really cursed that man out and told him she would never pay that money back to him."

Watching his mother struggle to support her four children ingrained in Sid a deep democratic belief in providing for those who have nothing. He knew his mother went on welfare the first year after his father died. He never forgot what that stipend meant to his family.

In 1950, according to the view at the time, Sid became a success. With the end of World War II, the bustling army training camp at Camp Butner had been emptied of its troops. The abandoned army hospital became a psychiatric hospital serving 16 counties, and a barracks was converted to Butner Training School. In subsequent years, the town housed a residential home for mentally retarded people as well as a school for the blind and several correctional facilities. It became a natural progression for many folks in southern Granville County to seek jobs in the new facilities that sat where their prime tobacco land had been just a decade before.

"For 18 years, I had been told that success was graduating from high school and getting a public job," Sid says. "Public job meant doing anything that you got paid for at the end of the week or month and not having to wait until the fall when you sold the crop of tobacco to get paid."

For Sid's mother, encouraging her children to pursue their education was critical, largely because she had never been allowed to pursue her own. "I think she was always mad because her father—he was a very prosperous tobacco farmer—he felt that the women's place was to grow up, get a husband, marry, have kids and farm. She transferred that anger about something she didn't have to make sure we did.

"She expected us to get an education, and at that time a high school education was a real achievement. I was the first one in my family to go to college, probably my whole extended family."

When his grandmother's farm sold in 1950, Sid's mother moved away from the piece of land that the family had lived on nearly all of Sid's life. Jeanette rented another farm and sublet it, making a small profit. She began working at the Murdoch Center, where she became food service supervisor. She was finally financially independent.

"I think she was brilliant in a way, had she had the chance." Sid still acts as his mother's defender.

I drive away today and think how it seems that Sid has lived his life as different as he could from his own daddy's. He's become something of a surrogate father to nearly a dozen men, primarily potters who passed through Cedar Creek. Many others who chose to pursue other avenues for their creativity found that sometimes while Sid sat and listened, smoking his Camels in front of the fireplace at Cedar Creek, they often figured things out for themselves.

It seems that he always remembered his mother's admonition to "never get above your raising," and he never lost the humility he learned as a child.

Chapter 4

Rich purple beauty berries glow like miniature grapes along the path to the gallery this morning. Today when we sit and fill our cups, I ask how his play is coming along. He calls it "Emma," and he's been writing regularly. She's a combination of three people, a spunky country lady patterned predominantly after Sid's 81-year-old lady friend who bequeathed him a kiwi vine when she passed away.

"I need at least three hours if I'm going to write," he explains.

He tells me of dialogue he's working on, laughs at his character's jokes and boasts that a production company is already interested in the piece. He's not throwing pots, and I worry it's because his swollen hands hurt. It must torture him if that's true, for Sid knew early on that he wanted to work with his hands. His interest in the arts had grown out of creativity spurred by the poverty of the times. That sense of frugality stayed with him. In his 70's, he still loves to search for the best deals he can find at yard sales and on eBay.

"I was always making something," he recalls, like the steps at his house. "I even bought the bag of cement." He cut pine off the farm to build hand tools, desks, night stands and whatnot shelves. His grandfather, Eaton Oakley, had been a woodworker, and he thought he might follow in his footsteps.

Sometimes, while the other children were playing ball on Saturday, he'd turn ice cream in a hand-crank freezer. He liked to bake cakes, but didn't like anyone to know about it. He tried crocheting for a time while he was at home helping his mother.

Occasionally he'd join in spontaneous fun with his cousins, making apple cider in a hand–crank cider press in a barn on the Ellis farm. They tossed crisp apples into the vat along with rotten ones, and they drank the newly pressed sweet juice.

Sid attended grade school at Stem School, which was expanded to include high school grades in 1922. The new brick building replaced the old wooden structure of the earlier school building, which was converted to a dormitory for teachers. The building was part of a county-wide effort to be more systematic about public schooling, and it served white children in Roberts Chapel, Knapp of Reeds, Tally Ho, Culbreth and Providence communities.

As a second-grader at Stem School, Sid didn't receive much encouragement about his ability in art. His teacher directed everyone to make Christmas cards except him.

"You don't have any talent," she told him.

"Maybe she was right," he says after thinking over the incident. "But maybe she said that to challenge me."

The morning that his teacher told the class to draw the Mayflower, he wasn't sure what she meant by the assignment.

"The only mayflower I knew was one that grew in the countryside and was called a maypop. It was real good for you."

When he realized everyone else was drawing a ship, he drew a ship with a flower and vine hanging down from its mast. That ought to cover all the possibilities, he thought.

But another of Sid's teachers left her mark on him as well. Principal James Broadus Haney had met Miss Bess White, a college-educated music teacher, and he felt his students needed to learn about music. The school couldn't afford to pay her, but he hired the young woman from Morrisville anyway, and she began teaching the children about some of the finer things in life. Haney paid a portion of her salary with his own money in order to offer this discipline to his students. Miss White, in turn, taught his daughter Lila how to tap dance, getting down on her hands and knees to help the tiny child make her left foot tap the right way.

Miss White was a pretty woman with brown eyes and long brown hair that she wore pinned up to make herself look older. She taught her students about more than music. From her they learned about culture and a world beyond the boundaries of Stem. And she left an indelible mark on Sid. In her, he found support for his appreciation of beauty and art at a time when his world revolved around tobacco and fighting the blight.

Haney was fired after only three years, not one to comply with political pressure. He went on to sell World Book Encyclopedias to surrounding schools. With his experience as principal, he knew that schools often had money left over at the end of the year, and if they didn't spend it, they would lose it. He convinced school officials to buy sets of his encyclopedias for the libraries, and each succeeding year he'd suggest they move those to classrooms and put a new set in the library.

Miss White continued teaching music to students at Stem School and piano lessons to private students, who sometimes failed to pay her. Whether she knew it then or not, she nurtured Sid's creativity with the musical activities she organized.

She taught the children ballroom dancing at school, and she organized dances so they could practice their skills. Sid's interest in the arts grew, and as a senior at Stem High School, Sid played the part of Dr. Hippocrates Joy, a 40-year-old psychiatrist, when his graduating class presented "Bolts and Nuts" in March.

When Sid graduated from high school in 1950, he started working at John Umstead Hospital, which he says resembled a dictatorship, an early sign of his propensity to buck authority and steer clear of the status quo. The hospital offered a unique opportunity to those in the surrounding area who had fought its creation in the beginning. After World War II, the War Assets Administration had phased out Camp Butner, and farmers who had originally owned the land bought back more than 20,000 acres. The North Carolina National Guard took about 5,000 acres to use for training, and more than 13,000 acres were transferred to the state of North Carolina in 1947. The transfer coincided with a push by John Umstead, Gov. William B. Umstead's brother, to provide better care for those suffering from mental illness. John Umstead Hospital replaced the old Army hospital, and it provided inpatient care for those with mental illness.

The sweet smell of thorazine permeated the hospital.

"That was the time before tranquilizers," Sid explains. "It calmed them down some. Every day, people got their shots of thorazine."

He earned $90 a month plus room and board for taking care of the patients, but he received no other benefits. He knew the salaries of supervisors of the hospital.

"I used to think, 'holy mackerel, what would I do with $600 a month?'"

And then Sid confesses: "I stole a mattress for my bed."

"My mattress was so hard, and I knew someone who had a key to the supply room," he pauses, then adds, "I didn't really steal it because it never left state property."

The next day the phone rang, and he was terrified he'd been caught, but it was only a supervisor asking him to work another shift.

In his first job at Umstead, Sid worked in the admissions ward, which was full of activity. He continued to give money to his family, and bought Hallie a yellow junior prom dress from his earnings. Later, however, he was assigned to a ward of patients confined to their beds, some of whom had had lobotomies.

"I could not handle people who were not up and about," he says. He only worked at Umstead for about 16 months.

"I left because I just knew it wasn't for me. I couldn't see myself doing this forever."

His older brother Sam was already in the service, stationed in Korea, and his younger brother Pete served in the Air Force in Japan.

"The Army was about to draft me, so I joined the Air Force. I didn't know much about guns. I figured I'd have to use less in the Air Force."

One of the few times he had to shoot his rifle, "the damn rifle fell apart," he laughs.

To me, sometimes Sid's foresight seems almost magical. Before he graduated from high school, he'd bought a used typewriter from the *Oxford Ledger* for $60 and taught himself to "hunt and peck." When he joined the Air Force, he went to basic training at Lackland Air Force Base, then Shaw Air Force Base in South Carolina. His superiors learned that he could type, so he was assigned to headquarters. The whole base was transferred to Germany, and Sid sailed there on the USNS General Leroy Eltinge.

His job was to account every morning for each member of the Air Force group at headquarters. There were six squadrons, totaling approximately 500 people. Everyone called him "Oak" and even then he was known for his generosity. He was so skilled in his work that other soldiers don't recall that he ever served guard duty.

He enjoyed traveling during his years in Germany. On weekends, he'd ride with his buddies on the training plane, visiting Denmark, Ireland, Scotland and England. They seemed to enjoy taking a country boy around and showing him the sights. The men took the train to Austria, Italy and France. He ate pizza for the first time at the Excelsior Hotel in Germany. He fell in love with Paris.

The Holland government paid all his expenses one week when officials invited him to visit, and a photographer followed him around on his trip. Sid later learned that the pictures and accompanying information were used in Air Force recruiting campaigns.

He figures he traveled to more than 15 countries. He saw the Mona Lisa at the Louvre on one of his excursions.

"I was expecting some huge painting," he says. "It's not all that large; it's just up on the wall."

In old black-and-white photos, he looks like a 15-year-old kid playing dress-up in his uniform, but Sid tells me he reached the rank of Sergeant Major, and he received an award for Airman of the Month. For that honor, he was required to march in a parade, but he'd neglected to sew his stripes on his overcoat.

"I did get called in for that," he admits.

Though he benefited from his years in the service, he still struggled with its rigidity. In one of his irreverent pranks, he was signing papers and joked, "I'm from the South," and put an "X" on his signature. Then he filed them away and forgot about them.

When he was promoted to Sergeant Major, his superiors found the forms, he recalls.

"Don't you think, Sir, that all sergeant majors should be able to read and write?" his superior said.

On occasion, when Sid and his friends had taken photos from their many trips to neighboring countries abroad, they'd have the slides printed and hold what they called a "premiere." He sent gifts home to his mother and Hallie. They loved the surprises, never guessing whether it would be Chanel perfume, an evening bag or maybe a clock or a mug. The Air Force offered him another promotion to reenlist.

"It was still too confining," he says, adding with his typical humor: "You couldn't be all you could be. At least I couldn't."

In his last six months in the service, his superiors asked him to organize a sports tournament with basketball, squash, racquetball and tennis for the whole European base. If he did that, they told him, they'd let him go home.

Sid was finally released three months early, so he could attend college. When he arrived home, he attended Campbell University on the GI Bill of Rights. He received $110 a month. At Campbell, Sid met Gordon Clark, another poor country boy who aspired to do something more than grow tobacco. Clark grew up in Harnett County, sure that he wanted to become an actor. He knew that Ava Gardner had grown up in nearby Johnston County, so he never doubted he'd be able to reach his dream. Clark and Sid took Spanish together along with Clark's roommate, Gordon Fearing. In 1958 the three were in the Collegiate Council for the United Nations comprised of students interested in international affairs. All three were in the drama society together.

After completing his two years at Campbell, Sid transferred to UNC-Chapel Hill where he obtained a BA in sociology and was a member of the Baptist Student Union, the Men's Honor Council and YDC. It was when Sid transferred to UNC-CH that he began to intentionally explore his interest in art. He had a friend who was an abstract oil painter, and he stretched canvases and sold those to art students to earn extra money.

Sid started taking art courses at UNC, where he preferred acrylics, which dried relatively quickly. "That was the one thing that saved me through art school. Working with oils, I always got them muddy."

He began reading about art. He read constantly. His work reflects strong Matisse influences, and he scribbled quotes he loved on pages in a manila tablet. He studied Cezanne, and he studied Braque for a whole year on his own. He painted vibrant flowers and portraits, but never was completely satisfied with his work.

Sid credits a creek from his childhood as an inspiration for his art.

"There was a creek over beyond our home, Rocky Ford Creek, that I practically lived on every minute that I wasn't working. I just absolutely knew that creek. I hope to get back down there one more time before I die."

I decide to visit the Rocky Ford. I believe it will help me understand Sid better; maybe it will touch me as it touched him. I call his cousin Tom Ellis to ask if I can cross his property, and he offers to take me to the old stream. I bring my camera so I can show Sid what it looks like now. Just in case the path is too overgrown for Sid to hike it. He's moving a little slower.

The creek sits at the end of a little-used path, barricaded by trees that fell during an ice storm in 2002. His cousin drives his Ford Pinto like a tank through the woods, crashing the downed branches aside. When he finally reaches the creek, still the sunlight shimmers on the water flowing over the moss-covered rocks, just as it did six decades ago.

The rich smell of leaf decay rests low in the air, just above the water held by creek banks perfect for hiding crawdads. An old path across the water led to Roxboro, and Sid found buckets of arrowheads along the banks.

Sid and his cousins often met there after completing their chores. For the youngsters, the creek provided a respite from the hard days of making do with what they had, yet instead of breeding despair, the poverty of the times spurred their creativity. With no extra money, the boys made their own toys winding tobacco stick strings around rocks to make baseballs, turning cow bladders into dodge balls, always aiming it at someone they loved during their school games.

No creative magic strikes me, but I recall the crawdads I caught in my own backyard creek, the Big Creek we called it. We'd walk barefoot through the water, stepping from sandbar to sandbar, scraping our buckets in the moss along the edge to see if we'd caught a salamander or perhaps a minnow. I remember the black snake that dropped from a tree, rose up cobra-like and circled like a periscope, watching us. It left my knees knocking, since I knew I'd have to cross back through the water where he swam if I ever wanted to return home. I was only 10, but I knew I'd in trouble if I stepped in the wrong place along the edge.

Chapter 5

"David called last night," Sid says after we clear the table and set our mugs down. "He was so excited. He saw his first bluebird of the season. It had built a nest in a bluebird box David and his kids made. He showed it to Lucas and Sydney."

Sid is proud that his son cares about seeing a bluebird, glad he's teaching that value to his own children. He tells me he spotted a big black snake in one of the old barns, and he tried to figure a way to catch it so he could save it for his grandchildren.

He's taken Lucas and Sydney to the Farmer's Market where they chose their own guineas and asked to sit in the back of the pickup truck on the way home to take care of the loud birds. Sid recalls the chicken he rescued when it fell off a 1,000-chicken truck into the middle of the road. He and a friend chased the bird through a yard and brought her back to Cedar Creek, proclaiming her to be Big Betsy, who later turned out to be the biggest rooster he'd ever seen. He tells me of the headless chicken that could walk and eat, and this I don't believe, but he promises to prove it to me.

For my part, I'm having an organizational problem at home. One of our cute little chicks grew into a rooster that attacked my son, and to my despair, he must leave our sanctuary. My sons' clothes don't fit in their drawers, and my laundry pile is growing of its own accord.

I find many more important things to do with my time than match socks and underwear with the correct child. I will paint my kitchen and feed my goats, play in the sandbox with my daughter or run with my double jogging stroller, but I cannot seem to fold the laundry. I struggle with details like whether to wash by color or category: should I put all the dirty socks and underwear in the same load, or should the black Batman underwear go in the dark load? I actually feel like an archaeologist investigating a find in sedimentary rock as I direct Jack and Michael to "look in the white layer for your socks." Sometimes I cover the boys with the clothes while they're searching, and they like that a lot. I'd even seen my dog April bury her bone in the pile.

Part of the problem is the logic of the laundry. With six people in our house, it seems like it would make sense to fold everything, then put the clothes away. I wash and dry until I can reach a stopping point, which, with six people, never comes.

"If you go to Duke Surplus, they have some nice dressers," he says. "They were nice wood, they were very reasonable, and you didn't have to refinish them."

He's bought several cabinets from Duke Surplus for his studio. "The next time you come, I promise I'll take you out there and show it to you. It's a real mess."

He's reorganizing the dust-filled studio. "I'm going to paint and write," he tells me, and then he changes the subject.

We talk about how he fell in love with Pat.

After attending two years at Campbell, Sid earned a degree in sociology from UNC-CH. He continued his schooling with graduate work there, and weekends he worked at The Lodge in Butner, earning a dollar for a Saturday night. A woman named Evelyn Clayton, called "Queen" by those who knew her, ran the nightclub.

One evening, Sid's friend Bob Thomas brought in a dark-haired beauty, who loved to dance. Pat Leveque asked Sid for a light.

He handed her an entire box of matches.

"Bob and I didn't get along much after that," Sid smiles.

Pat says that she had looked forward to an evening dancing with a group of her friends when she walked into The Lodge the night she met Sid.

"I wasn't dating anybody at the time. I just remember his eyes were very fascinating, very intriguing."

Pat's parents, Elizabeth Tuttle and Pierre Andre Leveque owned the Hotel Oxford, which they had purchased in 1937. Her mother was a poetess who graduated from Smith College. Her father was born in Paris and so was fluent in French, but he was also a student of many languages.

An elegant brick building with tall arched windows, Hotel Oxford held elaborate chandeliers, an elevator and a full-service restaurant. Rooms offered telephones, with air-conditioning that was optional. There was a television in the lobby, and the hotel was fire-proofed by automatic sprinklers. Cost for a double room was $3.50. The Leveques made a success of the hotel. The family attended the town's Baptist church because that's where business people went, and her father was a smart businessman.

Pat grew up in the family business, whispering in her home so as not to disturb the guests. The family originally lived in a two-room apartment in the hotel, but in her teenage years, Pat's room was on the mezzanine floor in one of the few rooms that her parents never booked. People in town viewed her as different. Sid himself didn't fit in a certain group, and he had developed a compassion for others who faced the same differentness. Pat's uniqueness attracted him.

In 1959, wearing long white gloves and a strapless full-skirted gown, Pat competed in the Miss Oxford pageant. She sang "Sweet Little Butter Cup" and took home the title and the crown. For Sid, 10 years her senior, Pat represented a level of sophistication to the farm boy he was. Sid and Pat began dating, with Sid driving to Oxford whenever he could borrow a car. One evening, he'd finagled his cousin's convertible to take Pat out. Driving home alone that night on Old Highway 75, he stopped the sleek car on the side of the dark road and danced.

"And I don't even like to dance."

In some ways, Pat seems more forthright than Sid, and she's shared a slightly different history of their success. I want to follow up with Sid.

"So Pat says you inherited money from her parents. That helped you with your vision for the gallery, I'm sure. How much did they leave you?"

"That's personal," Sid says. "I don't think we need to talk about that."

I stop myself from laughing and from saying, "Sid, I'm writing your biography. What could be more personal than that?"

That's probably when I realize, I've been manipulated. I've fallen in love with this 70-year-old man, with his story, with his spirit, but until now, I didn't recognize just how much of an editor he is.

That's also when I recognize that I'll continue to tell his story as he wants me to tell it, for as long as I can. I'm afraid I idolize him.

Sid and Pat both worked on their pottery techniques, however, Pat also took the lead role in caring for their two young children. At first they sold only their work at Cedar Creek, but gradually other potters they met asked if they could sell their work in their gallery. In 1969, Sid and Pat traveled to Brookfield Craft Center in Connecticut. They had signed up for a two-week session on advanced throwing techniques and agreed to split the time. The couple loaded David and Lisa into their car and headed north. Sid told "Slick the Bear" stories to the youngsters to make the miles pass faster. Slick was an amicable old bear

Sid invented whose antics never failed to place him into one sort of predicament or another, but he always learned a lesson at the end.

When the family reached Brookfield, Sid took the morning classes, leaving Pat with the children. In the afternoons when it was Pat's turn to study pottery, he'd take his turn watching the pair, often napping with them after their full mornings with Pat.

"You have such a huge responsibility," Sid reminds me. "Pat did most of the taking care of the two kids. She had a much bigger job than I did. You cannot have a more important job than taking care of those kids."

Sometimes I think the history he shares with me is meant to teach me more than what was important in his life. Sometimes I think he intends to teach me about my own. To tell him this story would probably sound petty, particularly since it pertains to the praise my husband receives for performing in public the activities that I do daily. The earliest example that I recall occurred during a family trip to the mall shortly after Michael was born. I left for 15 minutes to actually try on clothes. My husband sat near a fountain with Jack, then 2, who was in a stroller and fed Michael a bottle. Neither child cried the whole time I was gone, and several women stopped to say "how wonderful" it was to see a man taking care of the children like that.

This happens a lot. But the most recent episode amazed even me. I stayed home to paint the house, and my husband took all four children to the neighborhood swimming pool. For my part, I painted two walls with primer. He returned to tell me, "They were wonderful."

"I told them to sit with their backs against the fence and eat their snack because I was going to swim laps," my husband announced as I picked dried paint from beneath my fingernails.

"Two older ladies came up and said, 'Your children are so wonderful and listen so well.'"

"That's so annoying," I said, and he grinned.

The next day, I took all four to the pool in the morning. I'd brought balls and towels and toys. The same ladies were swimming laps.

"Walk!" I yelled.

"Mom, can I swim to you?" Michael asked. When he stood, he didn't reach above the three-foot level, but he swam like any lean fish would—about six inches below the surface. He needed a grown-up to stand in the water at the turn-around point.

Daniel and Kate, on the other hand, liked the baby pool. But I couldn't catch Michael in the big pool and watch the other two in the little pool.

"I'll let Michael swim to me 10 times, then I'll go back to the baby pool with you," I said in a relatively calm voice.

"That's not fair," Daniel announced.

And then I heard them. The ladies. "He had all four of them sitting and eating their snacks…," their voices trailed off.

I stuck to my plan, and it worked pretty well until Daniel ran and stubbed his toe, and Jack stepped off our chair and dumped Kate on the ground.

"Mom, it wasn't my fault," Jack explained.

"Everyone has to carry something," I said.

"Mom, can I swim to you?" Michael asked.

"No, we're going home," I told the four. I refused to look at the ladies. I didn't even glance their way.

For his part, Sid found time to take David and Lisa fishing at nearby Falls Lake, and he taught them how to make leather bracelets and clay pendants, macrame bracelets and tie-dye shirts. Sometimes he'd cut down a sapling, saw the trunk into disks and the children would sand the edges, polish them and hang them on leather cords around their necks. He helped David complete a school project on composting in one day, but it looked like they'd worked on it for two months. It was the 70's. David's hair grew long, and Sid left his untrimmed. Sid took Lisa to kindergarten in an old chalky green Chevrolet truck, and he'd pick her up and together they'd sing "Old 98" over and over and over again on the way home. Lisa sometimes went to work with him at the Alcoholic Rehabilitation Center. She'd see adults painting and tying knots in string. She peered over her father's shoulder as he taught the patients how to center their clay on the wheel.

The family always had dinner together, sitting down to talk with each other about their days. Sometimes, however, they had to nearly drag Sid back to the house, but it was a special time for the family.

Much of the youngsters' childhoods revolved around Cedar Creek. There were few boundaries between family life and work. Vacations to Florida were really trips to craft fairs, where Sid and Pat sold their work and David and Lisa wrapped pots and made change for customers. The children began calling their parents Sid and Pat because they didn't want to seem like the youngsters they were, as they made change and bargained with customers. David saw his friends whose parents worked 9 to 5 jobs, and he saw his father worked all day, every day. He saw that it was hard work, and his father was usually covered in clay dust. But he also saw that this father made things happen.

As Sid spent more time working with pottery, he realized he had talent, and he realized he loved clay. He'd spend hours covered in mud, smoking his cigarettes as the radio blared old Gospel hymns. "Will the Circle be Unbroken?" and "Amazing Grace" filled his studio.

No one tells you just how hard it's going to be to be married, Sid and I agreed. I admit I felt a bit cynical when I sat down in the pew at a recent wedding. I listened to all the traditional marriage love texts from the Bible, then saw the minister stand up to speak to this young couple who, I have no doubt, was clueless about what was about to happen to them. He told the couple that the love they'd just heard about really does apply to them, and he told them how. Then he warned them.

"First you fall in love, and that's such a wonderful feeling, with all the excitement, the newness, you'd do anything to be with each other, and each of you thinks the other is perfect."

"Then you are in love, and that's when you realize that you want to spend the rest of your lives together, for better or for worse. It's a pretty wonderful time, too, with many ways to grow together and learn about each other."

"There's going to come a time when you need to intend to love each other, and that's the part that's critical to the success of any marriage." He suggested that each spouse wake up and ask, "What can I do today to show my beloved love?" It's the closest I've ever heard a minister come to telling a couple of the rough road that lies ahead, even in the strongest of marriages.

For the Oakley family, everything revolved around the business. They lived at Cedar Creek, they worked at Cedar Creek, their social life centered around Cedar Creek, their vacations often coincided with craft shows to sell their pots. For Pat, who had grown up in a family business, that pressure took a toll. In 1988, she left Sid and moved to Chapel Hill. She didn't tell anyone in her family of her plan, most especially Sid. She feared he'd talk her out of her decision. They had both worked hard over the years to build what they thought was their future. Cedar Creek was starting to pay for itself, but instead of enjoying that success, Sid was always expanding and building something new. When she left, she thought she'd never come back.

Eighteen months later, Pat returned, but she did not resume her active role in the gallery. She set up a body-work and massage therapy office in her home and began seeing clients there. She'd finally found her own identity doing something she loved because she loved it, that was hers alone.

Sid, however, doesn't tell me Pat left him. Pat does. When we next talked, I tell him that what amazed me was that the two were able to find each other again. He only says, "I was a vegetable. I learned that I could take care of myself if I had to. You spend every minute of your time together, you need some space."

I could tell this must still be a painful memory for him, and he was editing me again. We moved on with our conversation. I recognized that I should ask more about this now, but I knew I wouldn't bring it up again.

It's almost summer, and he's wearing a long-sleeve shirt. He pauses longer between his responses. We've missed a couple of our weekly talks because of a conflict I've had, or because he's told me, "Next week would be better." I say fine and reschedule, and it isn't until later that I realize just how sick he's becoming.

We've been meeting for three months, and he finally tells me that he had a stroke just before I called him in December

"I never knew how important toes are to walk," he laughs.

I don't.

We plan to meet in a week to talk again.

Chapter 6

Today Sid wants to talk about his philosophy of art. We fill our coffee cups and sit down at the table before the fireplace, as is now our custom.

I'm frustrated that my oldest child has come home from school proud of his artwork, which he clearly traced for his teacher. Sid agrees that oftentimes teachers today don't allow children to be creative because they prescribe what's to be done and how.

"They're confusing being illustrators with what is really art," he explains. "I know that some of these people in schools are geniuses if they would let them be and encourage them to do it. It doesn't matter whether art is abstract or realism, that doesn't have a lot to do with if something is art or not. What I don't like is illustration called 'art.' Norman Rockwell, I have a lot respect for him as an illustrator. Timberlake is the same thing. He's a very good illustrator."

"Everybody has the ability to do pieces of art," he continues. "There's no right or wrong, but it's how you're feeling about something, not how it ought to be. Somehow there's magic in painting, and there's magic in pottery. I know that if we had good art programs, it would go a long way towards solving problems we're having in school. It gets them stimulated and interested."

At Carolina, Sid took a drawing class where he carried a huge sketch pad around campus looking for scenes to draw.

"That was the most successful class for me," he boasts. "I think it was about the only A that I made in college. Thirty percent of what was put on the walls was mine. My professor pushed and pushed and pushed me."

"There's a sense of creation when you're painting. If you really do something that's really good, you're not God, but you're god-like by creating something that's really good."

He again credits the Rocky Ford creek with his creativity.

"Maybe me and Pat and you and the kids and your husband could go to the Rocky Ford. I know they would love it."

I knew he was right. Our primary summer pastime has been catching frogs. I've tried to explain that you cannot hold a wild animal too long, or it may die. Michael caught a frog and carried it everywhere. He took it swinging with him, ensuring that the four-legged friend enjoyed the same twirling swing trick that he did. I stopped that activity. I'd be dishonest if I didn't admit to the battles that occurred because of who has a frog and who doesn't. And I know that if my neighbors can hear me—and I hope they cannot—they probably wonder when I command with a raised voice, "That's his frog, he had it first, give it back!" I know, I know, it's just a frog. But maybe you have to catch one yourself to understand the injustice of having someone catch yours if it hops through your fingers. I can't convey Daniel's triumphant, yet solemn, look when he walked up with a frog between his thumb and forefinger and announced, "Me caught a frog."

Last night, Jack helped his father cut the grass, Daniel practiced somersaults in the newly mowed lawn, and Kate strutted toward the goats. That's when I saw it. "Look Michael!" Immediately, he assumed the crouched position, quite resembling a frog himself. It hopped. He hopped. It hopped under some monkey grass, and Michael grabbed a second too late. "Do you want me to help you?" I asked, ready to corner it. "I can do it," he said, determined. I stepped back, he caught it and smiled. He allowed Daniel to look at it and pet it. I can understand why he wanted to cry when I made him let it go.

Sid went through cycles, at times preferring pottery, and other times painting. They provided different challenges for him. Painting was solitary, and Sid thrived by talking with people. He also felt frustrated because he wanted to be more abstract.

"I think there's an honesty if you're really painting not to sell, there's an honesty that you really do work for," he explains. "Like this play I'm writing is helping me to find a whole lot about this honesty."

I'd heard that Sid taught people potting lessons, and I want him to teach me, too. But I never ask. I can see that he moves more slowly each time we talk. He's writing more and painting again. He wraps himself in long-sleeved shirts and cradles his coffee cup to stay warm. I usually sweat.

In my high school art class, centering the clay was always hardest for me. It wasn't my lack of focus. I'd throw a ball of clay down on the wheel and wrap my hands around it only to have it thump, ca thump, ca thump into a lopsided lump that wobbled my arms back and forth uncomfortably until I stopped kicking the big stone that turned it. What I had to do was wedge my arms into the insides of my thighs and lean almost on top of my hands above the clay. It would become too dry, and little bits of sand would rub raw scrapes into the lower sides of my littlest fingers. When I added a little slip to dampen my bowl-to-be, I'd often get the whole ball too wet, the sides would collapse, and I'd have to toss it in the barrel and grab a new lump of mud.

"You can decide what kind of pot you're going to make before you make it. It's more a technical skill. In painting I never know how a painting is going to be until I get at least halfway through it. This is not unique or anything.

Other artists say this, you get about half way through it, and the painting begins to dictate to you because you're responding to what's already there."

Many times, he'd go to bed content with his painting, then wake up the next morning only to second-guess himself. He's only been satisfied a handful of times. One of those is his portrait of Lisa. "There's just absolutely nothing I would change about that portrait."

I am fairly uneducated about art. Sid shows me paintings in his Bonnard book. He loves the shimmering color.

"I have read and read and read. I love reading. I'm fairly knowledgeable about art in the last 150 years. It's just something that I choose to read. One time for a whole year, I studied nothing but Braque—that was on my own," he says. "I even tried to paint like him." He admired Monet, Cezanne, Van Gogh and Matisse.

"Here, why don't you take this home to look at it," he passes me the Bonnard book. "I've got another copy, so if I want to look at it while you borrow it, I still have one here."

At the ARC, he taught painting, woodworking and leather work. He experimented with batik, basket making, broom making, woodcuts and photography. He gave the residents blank paper, and he asked them to draw. He believed that if an alcoholic could have a sense of accomplishment, he might not go back to drinking.

I wonder if growing up with an alcoholic father helped him when he worked with the patients.

"My experience with my dad I don't think had any benefit of me relating to them. I had to relearn how to relate. It helped me accept him more. He was doing the best he could with what he had. And that's what I feel now."

The Oakleys lived in a small house provided by the state. It was full of toys and projects, a house holding love and creativity. Pat inherited many

Victorian antiques, but the couple found the formal furniture overpowered their tiny rental house, so they began selling those antiques from an outbuilding behind their home. It didn't take them long to realize that Sid could make reproductions of primitive North Carolina pieces. He crafted them out of pine, walnut and cherry, and they sold those in their outbuilding as well. Sid's mother Jeanette cooked big pots of Brunswick stew in the backyard, and Pat helped design the furniture, coordinating the colors and fabrics for Sid's woodwork.

As Sid worked on his program at the ARC, he expanded the media he offered patients.

He added clay.

It was not his area of expertise, but he thought clay would be a unique way to reach the patients. He spent hours reading about the process, and he began working with mud. The challenge of forming a functional pot out of the earth appealed to him. And he found he had a natural affinity for the medium, the cool, wet clay rising as he pulled the sides of a vase higher and higher.

He built a kiln, and he traveled to Seagrove to learn from the potters there who came from a long heritage of the craft. He visited Master Potter Ben Owen, Vernon and Pam Owens and Neolia Cole. He'd spend hours watching Owen refine his forms and asking questions about glazing, then he'd head back home. At work with his patients, he'd try out what he learned over the weekend.

"I always felt as an adult if you went to a hospital, and they stuck a little metal form ashtray in front of you and some precut tiles, I always thought that was kind of an insult, and so here we started with the raw materials in front of you."

"One guy said, 'Mud pies, I ain't making no damn mud pies.' I said look-a-here, if you can do this, what I'm going to show you, if you can do this, I'll shut up."

Sid started throwing a pot. "I tried to make it as tall as I could."

As he pulled the sides taller and the vase took its shape, the fellow grew quiet.

"You didn't have to do anything else to motivate him," Sid says.

In 1967, he wrote a grant to the National Institute of Mental Health that proposed using professional craftsmen in hospitals. The philosophy behind the proposal was that the real benefits of participation in any crafts were gained from a patient becoming involved with the material, and this could only happen when a creative approach was used. There were no attempts to interpret the patients' work. The concepts and philosophy did not differ from those of any good creative art program, but it was a unique approach for a hospital setting. It was funded for three years at $50,000 each year. When the grant ended, the state continued the program in its entirety.

He threw pots at home, firing them in a kiln wedged on their back porch, and he continued to learn more as he visited Cole Pottery and Owen's Old Plank Road Pottery in Seagrove. Owen had worked in Jugtown for 36 years before building his own studio. Sid was attracted to the style and design Owen was working from, which had an Asian influence. Many of Sid's own forms were reminiscent of the Chinese designs, as well as some of his glazes, like the copper red and crystalline.

He visited Vernon Owens on Saturdays in the 1960s. He'd drive down to learn or just to talk, and he was fascinated with candlesticks. Potters there saw him as a low-key man who knew a lot, as someone who appreciated the time they shared with him.

In 1968, Sid attended a two-week session on pottery design and techniques at Penland School of Crafts in the North Carolina Mountains. Hidden in the mountains of Mitchell County, Penland was founded by Lucy Morgan in 1929 as an outgrowth of a craft-based economic development program. Bill Brown, Penland's second director, added new media and developed more programs and scholarship opportunities. The school's creative

58

spirit permeates the hillside it hugs. There, Sid found an artistic community designed to nurture and refine students' creative abilities.

Officials from Old Salem approached Sid and asked if he would like to be the resident potter in the historic community in Winston-Salem. Though it would offer an opportunity to educate people about craft, Sid knew that he would not be able to be as creative, that he would be tied to the forms and glazes of that time. He and Pat declined the offer.

Eventually they bought land on the old Ray and Effie Sherron tobacco farm between Creedmoor and Butner, and named their dream "Strawberry Fields," borrowing the phrase from the Beetles' song.

On a Saturday afternoon in 1968, Sid was throwing pots at a demonstration at a local mall when Don Cohen stopped at the wheel and began talking with him. Cohen asked question after question about the forms, the glazing, building kilns. Sid, then 39, didn't take him too seriously. Cohen was 24 years old, just out of N.C. State School of Architecture. He offered to design Sid's house in return for pottery lessons, and Sid agreed to the deal. First, the two designed a place to work. The one-room studio was created from cypress, a shed 24 feet by 12 feet. Even in his early planning, Sid was always thinking of buying and selling. He enjoyed having people come in to talk, and he liked the educational part of pottery, as well. After completing the studio, Sid and Pat began building their home, and they slept there with a king-size mattress on the floor with nothing in the living room and dining room when they first moved in.

Sid took Cohen to Penland to talk with director Bill Brown because Sid was considering building a pottery school. Brown told them if he wanted to do pottery, he should do that; if he wanted to operate a school, then that was another story and might preclude much of his own work on pottery. Sid wasn't ready to give up his own creative time, so he decided to focus on the studio and gallery.

Once the kiln was working at Strawberry Fields, Sid and Pat would bisque fire on the back porch of their rental house in Butner, then glaze their work. Pat would unload the kiln on the porch, load pots into her car, then drive to their land and unload to prepare to fire again. Lisa, a preschooler then, would climb back and forth over the seat, occasionally cracking the wares in her scampering.

Pat first fell in love with hand building, using coils and slabs to build her pots, and later she concentrated on wheel-thrown pots. Sid began perfecting his wheel throwing. He taught craft workshops at area schools. In 1968, he led a senior citizens class at UNC-CH, and the next year he taught two semesters of beginning pottery at Allied Arts in Durham and two semesters of oil and acrylic painting at Durham Technical Institute.

From his beginnings in pottery and his reliance on Seagrove's master potters, Sid recognized the value of community among craftspeople, and through his work at Allied Arts in Durham he met other potters. In 1967 a group of 12 area potters put together a show they called the Triangle Festival of Crafts, and the success of that event spurred them to pursue beginning a craft guild. They did not, however, receive much support from other North Carolina guilds, which tended to be geographically segregated.

The area potters who had been interested in starting a guild met again in fall 1969 at Allied Arts and decided they were ready to move forward with their plans, in spite of that lack of support. Early on, Sid was an outspoken advocate for fair pay for good work.

"I think that this guild is a great idea," he said. "We need to have it, but not if it's based at this place." He'd been teaching at Allied Arts, and he felt they did not pay well.

The first Carolina Designer Craftsmen show was held in April 1970 in the old Educational Building on the N.C. State Fairgrounds in Raleigh. Water dripped through the roof, and the potters had to rearrange their booths around so that their work would not be damaged.

Though he enjoyed his work at the ARC, Sid preferred to be with people who motivated themselves. In 1974, with Pat's support, he stopped working for the state after 17 years. "Otherwise I was just going to wither up."

Making pots and selling pots became his full-time work. "It was great for about two weeks," Sid explains, "and then I began to get depressed. I was making a very good salary as director of the art program. The problem was I would spend days without anything to do. It's sad because I proposed all kinds of programs, and the staff would vote it down."

I've found an old photo of Pat in a psychedelic poncho. Sid's stooped next to her watching her hand build a pot. In another photo, a handwritten poster states: "Strawberry Fields is the name of our Craft-Pottery Shop. We do not have strawberries for sale." Eventually, the steady flow of bucket-toting customers who came looking for strawberries convinced Sid and Pat that it was time to change the name of their shop. Cedar Creek was born.

Freeman Beard, then art director for WTVD Channel 11 in Durham, designed the first logo for Cedar Creek, derived from a small branch that emptied into the nearby Neuse River. Once the dam was built, Cedar Creek became part of Falls Lake.

People began to recognize and look for Oakley pottery. Sid and Pat participated in the Carolina Designer Craftsmen Fair that would take place at Thanksgiving each year. They traveled to shows in Charlotte and Winston-Salem, and Sid met craftspeople whose work he liked. On those occasions, he'd ask the potters if he could sell their pots in his gallery. Instead of taking the pieces on consignment, however, he purchased the work outright, which provided not only a boost to other potters' morale, but also a financial boost. He knew good work when he saw it, and he would not have anything in his shop that he did not approve of himself. As the gallery became better known, potters and craftspeople started coming to him. Sid became the visionary in the business, and Pat the pragmatist.

"Pat's very good at the financial part, at details," Sid tells me. "I'm very good at looking ahead. It couldn't have existed without both of us."

Chapter 7

The yellow of the winter jasmine hints at spring on my walk down the path to see Sid, and Lenten roses open white, pink, magenta and purple. He leans on the counter, chats with Patrick and thanks him for the spaghetti sauce he's made.

"We've got coffee. Would you like some coffee? I'm going to change. Cream and sugar, I don't usually do it."

We fill our cups, then settle in our spot at the table in front of the fireplace. Patrick has just lit the logs, and they burn brightly before settling down to the low warmth from embers that will remain throughout the day. He disappears into the office. A quiet day in the shop.

I need to confess: "I cannot find anyone who will tell me anything about Mildred." We'd been debating calling one of her living white relatives, but we'd hesitated to stir up trouble.

"I've decided I'm going to call," Sid announces. "What can they do to me?"

He laughs and picks up the phone. I see a glimmer of the man who was known for saying what he thought. Sid makes the phone call while I stand near his counter. He dials the number, and I'm not sure if I ought to step away, but I really want to hear.

"This is Sid," he begins. "I've been looking back at some old photos, and I wondered if you could help me. Who were some of the girls in the class when I was in high school? OK, right, right."

"Something else. Do you know whatever happened to Mildred?"

"OK, well, then, thank you for your help with the class names. 'Bye now."

We walk back to our spot in front of the fireplace. "She said, 'Mildred who?'"

Sid looks disheartened, a little disgusted, mainly sad.

"We'll find her," he says. "We'll find her."

Sid hands me a fistful of 30 black pens labeled in yellow with "Make a click trip to the bank."

"I ordered these pens off the Internet."

They are simple pens, the kind that require steady pressure to write. Push the end in and out to extend and retract the point. A side piece to hook it to a shirt pocket. The innards rattle in the slender writing instrument. I always need pens.

"These are the best pens," he adds. "They write really, really well. They just feel good in your hand."

I thank him, then I hand him the pictures I'd taken of the Rocky Ford, of his grandmother's house, of the pack house. He looks at the Rocky Ford again. "It looks just the same as it always did." He promises to paint a picture of the old stream.

I've checked my notes at home and realized that up to now, we haven't talked much about his pottery or about how he learned his trade.

"Who were your mentors?" He doesn't answer my question as I expect.

"You do it if you like people. There were a couple of people that influenced me, and I was thinking back and Campbell University, although I didn't particularly like Campbell, their religious dogma--it was too strict. These were the fifties, you couldn't date unless you double-dated. There were some people who were really good teachers there."

Mrs. George Swann, who taught English Literature at Campbell, actually jumped up and down when he wrote a review of the choir that was published in the local paper. His biology professor Mrs. Philip Kennedy and his Spanish teacher Senorita Charlotte Mix guided him as well. Mix always had students who came to her room after class.

"All of these people taught me how unselfish they were by giving their time to help."

Mrs. Kennedy, the head of the biology department, gave him a job grading papers. She invited him over for lunch on the condition that he went with her to church beforehand. Never one to pass up a free meal, Sid went to church, then to her house for lunch.

"I looked forward to it, and I got over there, and she had white navy beans for lunch," he laughs. "I hate them--this is all I got to eat when I was growing up."

"She was so nice. She actually loaned me money so I could go to school."

He credits UNC Chapel Hill Professor Doug Sessoms with helping him with statistics. "I would've never got through grad school had it not been for Sessoms. There was just no way. He helped me through that."

"All these people had faith in people. They just demonstrated every day giving, giving, giving."

Sid carried that approach with him throughout his career and his life.

Hal Askins, the son of Frank and Ruth Askins, was only 14 the summer he went to help Sid build kilns at Strawberry Fields. To him, Sid was famous for starting the area's Little League, which evolved into the South Granville Athletic Association. Sid invited Dean Smith, who had just been named head basketball coach at UNC, to come and talk to the group.

Askins was too young to drive, too young for a work permit, so Sid hired him to help at the studio. His payment would be pottery lessons. Hal worked two jobs that summer. In the mornings, he rode his bike three miles into Butner to work in a greenhouse, and he'd bike home for lunch. After lunch, he'd hop back on his bike and pedal the six miles to Sid. He helped Sid build a wood kiln by stacking the brick and then his job became looking for wood, a monumental task since enormous amounts of wood were needed in order to keep the fire burning at a certain temperature for a certain amount of time.

Askins, who was the son of a minister, had generally tried to always follow the rules as a child growing up. When he began working with clay, he looked for rules in the craft to follow, but both Sid and Pat challenged him to be creative and to express himself through his work. When he considered pursuing pottery after high school, Sid encouraged him to go to college and, as his graduation gift, handed him a coffee mug with his handprint in the handle. Askins taught the first pottery class at Davidson College, and eventually became Special Deputy Attorney General for the N.C. Department of Justice.

Over the years, Sid and Pat developed an apprentice program, offering studio space for talented potters who had few resources with which to hone their skills in their craft. One of the earliest potters to take his turn at the cypress studio was Don Davis, who met Sid at Penland School of Crafts in 1974. Davis had just completed graduate school at Rhode Island School of Design and was looking for a place to work. Sid was taking a class, and he sought Davis out and offered him studio space when the gallery was still called

Strawberry Fields. He worked there from fall 1974 to mid-1975, with Sid refusing to let him pay for the gas he used in firing his work. Sid talked to him about folk pottery and traditional work being simple. In later years Davis understood that Sid had been talking about the purity of pots.

The young potter sought Sid's critiques even after he left the studio. He visited once or twice a year because he trusted Sid to tell the truth about what he was looking at and how he felt about it. Though they sometimes disagreed, Sid supported Davis's creativity. Davis never had been a traditional potter, and he learned he had to allow the purity of form to come through in his own way. With Sid, he felt a common purpose and empathy. Though Davis admired Sid's elegant forms, it was through Sid's paintings that he felt his spirit most clearly.

When Davis left, the studio space was open for another potter, and John Page moved in. Page had met Sid at a Carolina Designer Craftsmen fair in Raleigh. He taught hammock making at the Center for the Blind in Butner, but Page knew he wanted to work with clay. His stint lasted just under two years, and there he learned to make the pots he threw into his own signature pots. He moved on to his own studio in Seattle, and Sid sent him a little money to get started.

When Michael Sherrill was 24 years old, he traveled to the Fredericksburg Craft Fair with his boxes of functional salt-glazed pots. A straggly-haired hippie-looking fellow, Sherrill knew that then, the fair was a reach for him. He had grown up in Charlotte and learned in high school that he was dyslexic. Instead of continuing on to college, he had decided to pursue his pottery.

Sid walked up to him.

"So you're from North Carolina," he said. "I didn't think anything good came from North Carolina."

So began their friendship that lasted more than two decades.

The two began pulling his pots out of boxes.

"I really like your pots," Sid said. "I'd like to carry them in my shop."

He introduced Sherrill to the craftsmanship of folk potters through his Museum of American Pottery, a separate room he'd set aside because he felt it was important to teach people the tradition from which today's pottery came. He could have used the space for retail, but he was an advocate for education. He was provided an opportunity to further that mission by Dr. Walton Gregory and his wife Dr. Margaret Phluge Gregory, who had been instrumental in developing peanut strains suitable for North Carolina. They had been customers at Cedar Creek, and Walton Gregory shipped Sid 89 pieces of his pottery collection the day before he died. Sid used it as the foundation for the museum.

Sid and Sherrill talked for hours, and Sid listened, almost like a good professor. The young man felt a strong sense of support and could tell that Sid wanted to be a part of what was good. That faith from an established potter meant a lot. Sid struck Sherrill as a strong individual who didn't look for a lot of approval, a maker of his own path. A classic iconoclast, Sid was always looking at the edges to find his place.

For many potters, the winter was a tough time when galleries did not typically purchase work because demand was down. But Sid knew that was when craftsmen needed support the most.

"He bought my pots when I was hungry," Sherrill recalled. "He bought pots in the winter. For those of us who were trying to survive, he was a godsend. He was one of the ones who kept us alive year-round. He would buy in the winter time when he had to borrow money to do it."

Sid was drawn to fellow artists who shared his language. For the younger man, it was good to have his guidance. Sherrill sold his work at Cedar Creek for about 20 years until it became too expensive for Sid's gallery.

Kerry Gonzalez had been making his Raku crackle-glazed pots in primitive conditions in a shed without heat or running water. He met Sid at a show in Durham, and Sid invited him out to Cedar Creek. As he worked in the studio, Gonzalez saw Sid's generosity in dealing with potters who habitually had no money. He knew that Sid sometimes would send them $500 along with a note, "Send me $500 worth of pots when you have a chance."

While working at Cedar Creek, Gonzalez needed to buy a new vehicle. He'd found a van at a reasonable price, but he knew that obtaining a loan would be a challenge because he'd never had a credit card or loan. He asked Sid for advice, and the elder potter suggested he talk with someone at a specific local bank. After filling out the application, Gonzalez had asked when he might hear if he'd been approved. He was stunned by his good fortune when the loan officer replied, "You're approved."

When he paid off the loan three years later, he turned over the title to find Sid's name on the back, for he had co-signed the loan.

Sid's vision oftentimes seemed to be bigger than most other people's. When Gonzalez learned that fellow potter Lee Rosenbloom had cancer, he suggested that the six potters at Cedar Creek donate work and hold a benefit sale for their friend.

"No," Sid said. "It needs to be bigger."

Sid organized an auction, asking that the 350 craftspeople who sold work at Cedar Creek donate at least one piece for the benefit. He convinced a hotel to donate a ballroom for the event. Because his friend was too sick to attend, he carried a video and a sack of money out to the family after the auction.

Gonzalez saw that Sid was full of paradoxes. Even as he spent money for pots, Gonzalez watched the older potter straighten bent nails and reuse them. Sid feared fire, an almost paranoid fear that may have stemmed from a fiery car crash he happened upon on his way to Florida one summer. When Sid saw the car, he rushed to the blaze and pulled two people from the inferno before the car exploded. He didn't learn until later that another person had been inside. Still, the studio was filled with paper bags and newspapers to have on hand for wrapping pots, a veritable tinder box waiting for a match. In the late 1970's, there had been some miscommunication about turning off the burners for the gas kiln. When Sid went to turn on the gas, it exploded, knocking him backwards and blowing bricks 40 feet away, destroying the kiln full of pots, which were mostly Pat's.

Some of those who worked at Cedar Creek benefited more from the elder potter's philosophy lessons than from any pottery practicum. Bailey Hurt had gone to East Carolina University because he wanted to learn about ceramics and pottery. Sid called the college to find a couple students to hire, and Hurt loaded up his car and came to meet Sid at Cedar Creek on May 1, the agreed-upon time.

"There was nobody here," he said. Instead, he met John Page, who told him Sid would be back in three to four days. Hurt worked at Cedar Creek for several years, and the two men developed a close friendship. From Sid he learned, "You gotta have money. He doesn't believe in starving artists." Yet Sid also showed Hurt how important it is to have something to care about.

As I gather my papers and stand to leave, Sid pulls out a black-and-white photo. In it, he's playing guitar in front of Grand Central Station. He boasts that he earned enough money for dinner that night. It's an excursion he'd taken with Hurt several years before.

"I didn't know you knew how to play guitar," I say.

"I don't," Sid laughs.

Chapter 8

I've already confessed about the pot Sid gave me. I know I shouldn't keep it, what with a potential conflict of interest and my need to be reliable and honest as a writer. It's light and smooth, but sturdy and shapely. It bulges out like a ball, and the crystals explode in shiny pearl gently on its sides. It's cool and comforting. I always hold it with two hands; one wouldn't be quite safe enough for its size. What I haven't shared is the letter inside it. The day before my birthday in 2002, Sid wrote a letter thanking me for the little story I'd written about him and the gallery. He wrote, "…I think it was one of the very best articles that has been written about us. It was honest and it captured the feeling of the place…." I still blush when I read it for not only was Sid's generosity legendary, but so was his tendency to proclaim something "the best."

Our cups are full, and he preaches his mantra.

"The important thing is to focus on something and totally forget about how much money you might or might not make because you've got to truly focus on something you truly love to do," he says when we meet this morning. "I really believe that. It's been true for me. It could be true for anybody I think. You find what you want to do and learn all you can about it. It's too sad to be 65 and say, 'I could've done it if I'd've just tried.' If you try to do it and you fail, you're not really a failure because at least you did try."

As a freelance writer, I'd never figured my hourly rate because it could have convinced me that my efforts were not being well compensated. Instead, I chose to focus on the writing of the story. I simply love the writing. I love my dictionary and my thesaurus. I didn't tell Sid that, but I suspect he'd already figured this out.

Sid appreciated creativity wherever he found it, and he supported those in whom he saw a passion for their craft, whatever it happened to be.

A mason for 50 years, Burnice Sparrow calls Sid one of his best friends. He built Sid's basement, and when he finished the job, he handed Sid $50 he'd saved on the job. Sid gave the money back to him, and from then on he called Sparrow whenever he had a masonry job. When Sid decided he wanted a large fireplace in the new addition of the gallery, he called Sparrow. The fireplace consists of more than 800 old oversized bricks from Carr Mill and more than 300 other bricks from a retirement home in Efland.

"This is your space, do what you want to in here," Sid told Sparrow, and the mason started working. Sid peered over his shoulder, commenting that it looked, "too big, too big."

He constantly chided Sparrow, "I don't know whether that thing's going to fall down or not."

Over the years, Sparrow baked Sid pineapple-coconut cake. He'd bring his friend his 14-day pickles and stop by with sacks of wine sap apples. He appreciated that Sid, "was just plain as an old shoe. I never knew him to ever wear a suit of clothes. He didn't put on no airs."

Sid found people, all sorts of people. He listened, and he encouraged. Bleached-blonde and purple-clad, Lou Proctor had been a customer since the 1970's when her mother-in-law helped her find the gallery. In 1985 she stopped in one day and talked to Sid. She had been unhappy working at her job at

Craven County Industrial Development Commission. They sat smoking in front of the fireplace.

"Why don't you quite that damn stupid job?" Sid challenged her. He promised to bring his own work and that of a few other choice potters to help her begin an art gallery with her friend Nancy Ward. The women bought business cards, though they had no business, but they named their venture "ART Gallery, Ltd." In 1986 they found the corner on Pollock Street in New Bern and began selling work from 16 artists.

Sid and Proctor shared business strategies, and they enjoyed smoking, chatting and joking with each other. She'd call him and wake him up during his nap; he'd leave messages on her answering machine insinuating that she wasn't working. Proctor knew that Sid believed art ought to be affordable to the public. In 1989, he convinced her to judge his National Teapot Show. They met, along with Pat and resident potter Brad Tucker, at a hotel in Goldsboro halfway between New Bern and Cedar Creek to judge the show, reviewing slides in the hotel restaurant. They traded art, and they traded pranks, and Sid gave her books and paintings and pots over the years.

"I was always his best friend," she says, though she herself admits that many people could say the same. She knows it does not diminish the truth of their friendship.

When Ben Owen III graduated from college, Sid wrote him a letter of encouragement and offered Owen one of his first shows, providing the young man a chance to put together a body of work for an exhibit. Though he treasured the tradition from which he came, the opportunity for Owen to be in a different environment and Sid's encouragement meant a lot to the young potter. Sid saw that Owen had the focus he needed to be able to do the style and design his family was known for.

Owen was demonstrating pottery at his show at Cedar Creek in 1994 when Sid walked up and watched for a while.

"Ben, I want you to make one of those candlesticks for us," he requested. The form was a signature shape Owen's grandfather had made in Jugtown and one that Vernon Owens still makes today.

"Now slow down, don't do it so fast. I want to see how you're doing all these different things with your fingers."

Sid watched, then ambled into his studio and tried to make one himself. He returned later and said, "You know, that really worked a lot better for me after I saw you make it."

Over the years, Owen would occasionally stop to visit Sid, or he'd receive one of Sid's trademark handwritten notes.

When Sid traveled to craft fairs, he'd see new potters sitting at their booths full of pots, hopeful they'd sell their work. He'd trade or give them something, and sometimes he'd buy a few pots to encourage them. George Griffin says he was one of those potters. In 1982, he was at a craft show in Maryland, admittedly feeling a little ignored, when Sid stopped by his booth. He complimented Griffin on his functional stoneware, and talked with him for a while, then as he walked away and was at the edge of his display, Sid turned around and said, "I'll take $50 worth." Griffin never forgot what that gesture had meant.

Sid's Seagrove teachers continued to keep up with him over the years. Though Vernon and Pam Owens didn't visit often because both families were consumed with their businesses, Sid sent notes on occasion, or if Tucker traveled to Seagrove they'd send Sid their regards back with the young man. Sid always asked Pam to submit a teapot for the National Teapot Show, which she says she appreciated because oftentimes her work was overlooked.

"Y'all make great pots and just don't get much credit," Sid said. Yet he was bothered by other people who took themselves too seriously, and he'd quip, "Well, that's not necessary."

When the Owens's son Travis was about 5 years old, he [...] Creek with his parents.

"Travis, tell me about those face jugs you're making now," Sid said. Travis explained what he'd done to the pot. Sid pulled out one of his own pots. Travis recalled Sid asking, "Want to trade?"

But Sid was attracted to more than reaching the visual and tactile senses. He also loved music, and he sought ways to incorporate that creative medium into Cedar Creek.

Jack LeSueur had first met Sid in 1974 when Sid was awarded a grant from the N.C. Arts Council for his ARC project. He and his wife Pattie began performing bluegrass and ballads in the mid-1970's, and Sid noticed them at the Carolina Designer Craftsmen fair at the State Fairgrounds. In the early 1980's, he hired the couple to play at Cedar Creek for its biannual kiln openings. They played in front of the fireplace, and the bathroom kept clogging up. The regular gig was a symbiotic relationship. It gave the LeSueurs exposure, and Sid always told them it boosted his sales. In the early days of the kiln openings, they'd serve wine. That stopped when Pat realized just how many pots Sid was giving away after drinking a glass or two.

"Oh, this is beautiful," Pattie said to Sid.

"Take it, here, take it," he told her, as he handed her a crystalline vase.

When Brett Stolp had moved from California to go to medical school at Duke University in Durham in 1979, he felt like he'd entered another world. He'd grown up with a mother who was an artist, and he was just plain homesick. He found Cedar Creek and Sid, and the two spent cold winter evenings sitting in front of the fireplace sipping wine from coffee mugs and talking. Brett's wife Janet, a musician who was named North Carolina's 2003 Singer Songwriter of the Year, performed at Cedar Creek. When their first child was born, Sid pronounced himself Ryan's godfather, and when the child was old

wheel, he taught Ryan how to throw a pot. They

sson he taught: to value the process of creating

the joy of doing it, but also not to fear the outcome.

nonica Bob" Waldrop called Sid to see if he'd be

Sid appreciated harmonica playing and always said he was

going to ___ o do it himself, and he invited the musicians to play without

ever hearing them audition. "Harmonica Bob and Near Blind Jim" played blues and gospel music from black musicians of the 1920's to 1940s, and when Sid paid them he said, "You were exactly like I thought you would be." They honored Sid with their tune "Sixteen Pots," to the tune of "Sixteen Tons" by Merle Travis's 1949 hit.

Years later, Waldrop was performing at a wedding reception, when the caterer told him her story of Cedar Creek. She had stopped in the gallery and picked up one of Sid's pots and commented to a friend how beautiful it was. When she saw the price she added, "I just can't think of buying this. I haven't worked much lately and am barely squeaking by right now."

As she went to put the pot back in its place, she sensed a presence behind her. It was Sid, but she had no idea who he was. He snatched the pot out of her hands and said, "Give me that!"

He looked at it for a moment, handed it back to her and said, "I'm Sid Oakley, this is my business, it's my pot and I want you to have it. Here. Now you enjoy it, and thank you for coming all the way out here to see our stuff."

Then he walked away.

Sid met Don Paterson when he stopped by the shop and showed Sid a silver chest he'd crafted out of hickory for his wife. Paterson was an engineer by trade who helped establish the Micro Computing Center in Research Triangle Park. Shortly after moving to Raleigh in 1980, he bought a radial arm saw to pursue his interest in woodworking. He soon found he had a talent for the craft.

"I want to sell these," Sid said. "It's near Christmas--can you make 50?"

He sent Paterson e-mails that challenged him to improve upon the design of the Shaker style furniture that both men loved.

Sid's indomitable curiosity and enthusiasm sometimes led him to ideas that weren't so lucrative, however. For example, Sid decided he wanted Paterson to make bird houses. The reason? Sid had bought brass washers on the Internet.

"They'll be perfect for a bird house," Sid explained. "This'll be the door."

The gallery was a way for Sid to obtain work, to spend time with it and to decide if he did in fact really like something. Part of the whole concept of Cedar Creek was having people around him, and he structured it so that it was his own kind of country club. He met all kinds of people, and there was always somebody who wanted to eat lunch with him.

Like many of those who met Sid for the first time, cardiologist Marty Sullivan claimed he could make the pots that Sid suggested when, in fact, he could not. He appreciated Sid's commitment to art, and he saw how Sid protected his world. One day near Christmas Sid and Sullivan were in the studio throwing pots amid shelves of crystalline pots, and a big executive walked up the path.

Sid scrambled to put the pots away. The man walked in and said he had an important client, did Sid have anything?

"We're all out," Sid told him in his best deadpan. "Call back, and I'll see what we can do."

Just 10 minutes later a widow came walking up the path, and Sullivan watched Sid hurry out to hand her a crystalline pot.

"Here, I want you to have this," he said.

"Sid, I can't afford this," she replied.

"Why don't you make me a pecan pie?"

Chapter 9

I meet him outside the shop today. He's spent the afternoon with his newest granddaughter, Emily. Lisa walks up, and Sid boasts, "Watch this!" He faces the infant and says, "Smile," and she does.

It's late afternoon, and I tell him about my visit with his son, David. He's shared a few tales, but nothing that will help me balance my idealized version of Sid.

"I need to find out about your faults," I say. "No one is going to believe you're perfect."

"I drink too much coffee," he grins, "and I've smoked too many cigarettes."

Most everyone I speak with about Cedar Creek wants to tell me they know Sid. Even in casual conversation they want to tell me he's a friend of theirs, whether they are customers or salespeople, they all feel a connection to this man. Sid never passed himself off as a sophisticate. The comfortable country talk was genuine, but what threw people was that they didn't expect someone from the country to be very smart or to be very literate or to be very worldly. Sid never felt that he couldn't do something, and he was wise enough to surround himself with people who would energize him and enable him to accomplish what he wanted.

I'd driven to Seagrove to visit his mentor Vernon Owens. I met Bruce

Gholson, and Ben Owen III photocopied a letter that Sid sent him years ago. I got carsick on the twisty drive to Michael Sherrill's studio in Hendersonville, and I made a few wrong turns before I found Blaine and Laura Avery at a show at Frances Alvarino's garden. The couple remembered when Sid gave them a month's free rent during an especially challenging winter. I invited myself to the homes of Jan Gregg, Pepper Fluke and Paul Minnis, folks who had known Sid early in his career. I called Don Cohen in Massachusetts, John Page in Seattle and Don Davis in Tennessee to understand what it was that Sid did for them. I e-mailed his buddies from the Air Force, and I visited Gordon Clark, his college roommate who lives south of Pittsboro. I met a cardiologist for coffee, and Sid's minister friend showed me his baptism certificate. I brought a plastic-corked bottle of wine purported to be delicious to a dinner party with a group of folks who had worked for a decade together at Cedar Creek. I rented a hotel room in New Bern and spread my notes along the entire floor before meeting with Hurricane Lou Proctor at her art gallery as she pulled paintings and pots and dusty handwritten letters from Sid and fought back her tears.

Unfortunately, those travels had done nothing to dispel my idolatry of Sid. But I sit for hours and talk with those who knew him best, who loved him the most, and they are the ones who saw the imperfections that made Sid human. As Pat said, "All heroes have feet of clay."

Sid could be gruff, and he could be abrupt. At times he grew tired, and he worried more than he allowed most people to see, for creating the magic of Cedar Creek took considerable energy. Not all of his ideas made sense, like the path to a kiln he asked his friend to tear out and rebuild just because he wanted a curve in the walkway. Built to his specifications, however, the path made moving pots much more difficult. He liked to be in control, and though he sought those who could help him move to another level if he felt stuck, he was quick to rein them in and reassert his presence once they had accomplished what he needed.

Although Sid liked to debate for debate's sake, he didn't like to be confrontational when it came to decisions about running Cedar Creek. Sometimes if there was a disagreement, he'd simply leave. Oftentimes before the kiln openings he wouldn't be around when there were key decisions to be made. He hired people who were comfortable making those decisions, but he didn't hesitate to second-guess them if he felt they were wrong.

He became angry at all women during the months after Pat left him, but he struggled to learn why it had happened. He didn't seek out anyone to replace her; in his eyes, no one could. He opened a shop in Raleigh to make it easier for folks to buy Cedar Creek wares, but it didn't take long before he recognized that the magic of the gallery came from its unique location in the middle of the countryside, a day-trip destination in itself.

Cedar Creek became Sid's kingdom, and he its king. As his acclaim spread, young potters looking for guidance came to him, and he continued to find promising potters who needed a boost, whether it was simply needing equipment for their craft or spiritual encouragement. Sid thrived on the energy of the young people with whom he surrounded himself. When he needed work done, he'd call someone he knew because he trusted his friends.

In the early 1980's, Sid's crystalline glaze attracted the attention of officials from the Smithsonian Institution, who asked him to make a series of pots for its catalog. He made 186 pots in a difficult form with crystalline glaze.

"I loved doing that," he recalls. "You come up and work a day, and you look back and see a day's work."

Brad Tucker had just finished school and was looking for a place to apprentice when his friends told him about Cedar Creek and Sid. He'd obtained an English degree, then studied pottery at Montgomery Community College and was doing research for the N.C. Department of Public Instruction. When Tucker arrived at Cedar Creek, he knew immediately that he wanted to stay. Sid and Pat decided to give the young man six weeks. Sid was busy with the

Smithsonian crystalline pots, and he didn't have a lot of time to spend with Tucker when he started work the first week in June. He set Tucker up with a wheel in a corner of his own studio, handed him a pot and asked him if he could make 100 a day.

Tucker had answered, "Sure, no problem," but he admits now that he couldn't have made five.

Each morning, Sid would give Tucker an assignment. He'd take a pot from the shop and say, "Make me 50 of these." At the end of the day, he'd come back and sort through them, trying to find one that he could praise. Often he'd throw everything out.

Sid was a workhorse. He watched the shop every single day, including weekends. On Mondays, it was closed because Sid was throwing pots. He always had something for Tucker to do, even if it was just, "Let's move this over there" for no reason other than Sid thought it should be done. When, in 1982, Tucker decided he wanted to travel to Penland to gain training and to have some space away from Sid, Sid gave him $400 toward tuition for a two-week session. They agreed that when he returned, he would no longer be an apprentice. When he came back to Cedar Creek, Sid and Pat gave him his own studio, which had been Sid's old office.

Tucker was thrilled to have his own space, and he worked hard to straighten the shed and build shelves. He paid $50 to cover the fuel he used. They agreed that he would only be paid for that which he sold. Sid would pick out a pot, and he would look at it and pronounce: "Now this pot has life to it." Though Tucker wasn't sure what it meant at the time, he was thrilled with the praise and the fact that it meant he'd receive a dollar, and every dollar mattered as he struggled to make car payments and pay bills.

The two worked together on some pieces, with Tucker throwing the pot and Sid carving the designs. Together they looked at pots and studied them. Sid often talked about "an honest pot," where the craftsman was being true to himself, not trying to stretch boundaries. They both valued remaining true to tradition, and though Tucker sometimes experimented with what he calls "artsy pots" he'd usually end up taking off all the extras.

He valued Sid's critiques, though sometimes they could seem harsh. Potters like Sherrill and Davis also sought Sid's comments even when it wasn't always what they wanted to hear. For these potters, the value came from Sid's honesty, and they knew that when he said he liked something, he meant it.

At times, Sid would talk to people, and he'd see not so much a flaw in their work as just something he didn't like. Others in the shop often couldn't see what he was talking about, even when Sid espoused, "There is nothing really original; their work is just not original."

Other times, Sid took thoughtful care to comment, as was the case when a pottery family sent him a box of pots to sell. The pots were of poor quality, and Sid wrote a long letter detailing what was wrong with the work. It was very constructive criticism and included the question, "How can you sell this stuff? Where is your sense of pride?" They did not react well to his well-intentioned advice.

For Sid and Brad, the days developed a kind of rhythm. Most days, the two would meet at the shop at 10 a.m. and sit outside to talk. What began as a teacher-apprentice role developed into a deep friendship, and the men sat and talked about pots every day over a cup of coffee while Sid smoked his Camels. Though the details in the daily routine changed over the two decades that Tucker has worked at Cedar Creek, they still sit outside talking about pots. As Sid hired more people that he trusted, he distanced himself from the daily decisions. But whenever he felt out of the loop, he'd be quick to step back in.

When Tucker outgrew the small studio, Sid offered to help build him another, and he and Pat gave the young man a small plot of land along with it. Sid took out a napkin, as was the typical way he designed his new projects, and Tucker drew exactly what he wanted, which was a 500 square-foot studio.

"That's not big enough," Sid said. "If you're going to spend the money to do it, it might as well be a bigger studio."

Sid met John Martin when he worked at a nursery in Raleigh, and the two became friends. When Martin left his job there, Sid hired him to oversee the gardens at Cedar Creek. But he also knew that Martin, a college-educated chemical engineer, could help him refine his glaze formulas and make them more predictable. Sid was already firing copper red, and he'd found that the right amount of smoke was critical to the final glaze. But the chemist helped Sid with turquoise blue. Sid had always felt his tone was too green, but when they added a little lithium, it increased the blue in the glaze.

Martin also helped with some of the research for Sid's crystalline glazes, as did a California potter. Sid tried for two years to make the zinc crystalline glaze work and had found that the timing of the smoke was critical in crystal formation. Sid was intuitive in his creativity, and he used Martin to help him tweak the formulas and make them more consistent. Once he figured out how to do something, he became bored.

In some cases, when Sid saw his protégés exceeding his own abilities, he'd begin butting heads with them. But to those who shared the long hours with him at the gallery, he'd remind them, "You need to be able to tell me to go to hell."

Patrick Hurley's mother first brought him out to Cedar Creek when he was 10 years old. When he graduated from N.C. State University, he wasn't sure what he wanted to do, so he called Sid to see if he could bring his pots out to show him. Sid looked at the pots and said, "Lord." Later he told Hurley he wasn't interested in seeing his pots, he was more interested in seeing his feeling for pots. He told Hurley he'd work with him for a couple of weeks during the summer. It was May 1993, and Hurley worked for two weeks in the shop. Sid never mentioned his time was up. One day the grass needed mowing, Hurley worked a couple Saturdays, and the two weeks turned into 11 years. What stood out for him was that Sid always showed him that he was appreciated, and he never took anything somebody did for granted. He recognized hard work and compensated those who helped him not just monetarily but verbally.

Hurley watched as Sid helped people, all sorts of people, not just potters. Not everyone appreciated what he did, but that didn't stop him from helping others. Hurley warned Sid that people were taking advantage of him, and the elder potter replied, "Well, you know that's not going to stop me from wanting to help people.'"

Hurley cared for Sid as he would have his own grandfather. He'd make spaghetti for him and BLT's. He often brought him lunch and made him coffee in the morning. Sometimes he'd have Sid and Pat over for dinner at the little house he rented from them.

He told Hurley, "Love yourself and be honest with yourself, and the rest falls into place." He wouldn't tolerate discrimination of any sort.

On Sunday mornings, the two would head out to local flea markets, for Sid collected everything from tin lunchboxes to CD's. Sid loved fruit and the Buckhorn Flea Market had a big produce market, and they frequently stopped there. Some days they would go on what they called "excursions" where they would eat lunch somewhere, and then go to a record store or book store. They searched through junk shops and thrift stores.

Hurley and Martin joked, "Sid would buy a hysterectomy if he got a good deal on it."

Sid frequently searched the Internet looking for good deals. If he saw something on sale that he knew a friend of his collected, he'd buy it. He loved yard sales and he hoarded things. His purchases over the years ensured the shop would have pencils and pens to last forever.

Sid's reputation grew. He became more confident and sometimes a little cavalier in his critiques of some of the potters who looked to him for guidance. In some cases, Sid rubbed potters the wrong way, and a few still harbor bad feelings from off-the-cuff remarks he made at the height of his career. One potter brought black pots with white glaze splashed over the outside. Sid was talking to him by the fireplace and told the young man exactly what he thought in terms that were crude, but honest, and the young man was mortified. He never sold work at Cedar Creek again.

Sid liked public recognition, and those around him felt that he never received all that he deserved. When the N.C. Mint Museum held its show featuring crystalline pots, many of the potters he'd taught the skill were invited to display their work, but Sid was not mentioned. Even so, those around him could see that he was taken more seriously than he thought he was.

In spite of the growing acclaim and respect Sid obtained, he still felt it was important to share with me the memory of a second cousin who came by the shop and said, "I haven't seen you in 25 years, and I want you to know, we are so proud of you."

Chapter 10

Afterinterviewing Sid and Pat for the first story, I'd called back
several times to clarify certain facts or spellings. For one thing,
he'd told me the name of his shop was Cedar Creek Pottery and Gallery, not
exactly a flowing phrase in my mind, and I thought I must have misheard him.
I'd written the best article that I could at the time, and I sent it to the
newspaper, and I'd told Sid when his story would run. When the newspaper
held it, as they are prone to do, I called to explain to him what had happened.
"It didn't have a deadline," I explained, and it could run when they needed it to.
He didn't seem bothered at all. When the story ran, it had been placed not on a
section front as I'd anticipated, but on the inside of the arts section. I called Sid
again to apologize.

"I think it was just where it needed to be," he said.

It was only a $50 story, and I felt a little foolish that I cared about it as
much as I did. But when I talk with Sid today, I realize that he didn't think I was
silly at all.

"Art is really something that really keeps you going and is so hard," Sid
says. "Sometimes you wish you were just a ditch digger, and somebody's telling
you how wide and how deep. Then you entertain the thoughts for about two
minutes. It is tiring, but it's on the opposite end of that too; it is invigorating at
the same time. I also think that art is 1 percent talent, and 99 percent hard

work--that's what Matisse said. You can't get ideas by thinking about it. You've got to get ideas by working on it."

Sid knew that, for me, the 15-inch story on the inside of the arts section was my art.

"I think art is sort of a wider thing than something on canvas," he continues. "It's also a total way of life. I'm not unique or I'm not different. It's just that I've had opportunities."

What I had come to see, though, was just how adept he was at creating his own opportunities. He knew how to create excitement about whatever it was that he was doing, and he was as masterful at that manipulation of the market as he was of the pots he threw. In some ways he reminded me of my husband who had convinced our four children that he was the best cook around.

Don't think I'm ungrateful. I truly appreciate the times my husband offers to cook dinner for our family, and I'll admit it: I lack the predisposition to attempt culinary accomplishments.

Maybe for me it's because it generally takes less than 10 minutes for our family to consume a fine dinner, if I am ever so inspired to prepare one. And truth be told, Daniel is just as happy with hot dogs or canned spaghetti as he is with one of my meals. Michael, like me, enjoys eating cereal, which we have for dinner only on special occasions.

Tonight my husband called to tell me he was going to make potatoes for dinner. I suggested we have eggs and French toast, but he really wanted to make his special potatoes, so I acquiesced.

But as I watched him chop his potatoes, slice his onion, dollop his margarine, salt and pepper the pile, then stick it in the microwave and announce, "These are going to be the best potatoes," I couldn't help but wonder at the difference between us.

He began singing a song about how delicious his potatoes were going to be. This no longer fazes our children, who simply continue on with their conversations as their father dances to the melody only he knows.

When he placed the pot on the table, he grandly removed the lid. Steam whooshed dramatically as it escaped, nearly singeing Michael.

"These are so delicious," he announced again, which by now, I'm growing weary of hearing. "They are so good," he added as he heaped another spoonful on his plate.

"I don't like onions," Kate announced.

"Kate thinks they have germs," Daniel explained.

"They do," she pouted.

"Then pick them out," my husband said. "I'll eat them. I love onions."

I watched as he grandly added no-salt seasoning mix, then sprinkled the mound with cheese. "It needs to gently melt to add to the ambience," he noted with a flourish of the cheddar shreds.

"I could have made potatoes, I would have loved to make potatoes," I told him.

"I really am an expert at this," he said, with a hint of compassion and a touch of condescension.

I'm not above admitting that everyone enjoyed his meal. I'm not even all that jealous of his success. I've learned his secret, you see, because he told me, "The secret's in the sizzle."

Sid knew that, perhaps better than anyone. He created a mystique that made writers want to write about him, his shop and those who worked there. When there was an uproar about lead in the glazes on pots, Sid was quoted as the authority on the science of the subject, even as he reassured customers that Cedar Creek pots carried no such poison. He'd take opportunities to publicize his protégés, as he did in 1989 when he told a reporter about Jim Lux: "Jim doesn't talk much, but you're going to hear a lot from him…He's extremely talented, very hard-working, very sensitive to everything around him." A few days later, Lux won first prize in the Wake County Artists Show.

Sid made his twice-a-year kiln openings seem newsworthy again and again, and eventually the name of the event became a metaphor for the craft festival. Yet he kept the name to tie it to the heritage of the craft and the excitement that accompanied the new work that would still be warm on the shelves when he or Tucker unbricked their kilns. The story I wrote I'd pitched as newsworthy because Lisa was taking over the helm of the business, but I didn't know then that Sid had handed it to her at least twice before, only to take back control when he decided he'd had a long enough break.

The gimmicks he found for his kiln openings were as creative as the work he featured. In his old undated letters announcing the events, he exclaims over white oak splint basket exhibits and blown glass perfume bottles. He writes of woven pillows, handmade paper lampshades, wool rugs and clay drums. He names the products: Don Francisco brass key rings and bells, Ray Memmel belts and buckles, Eric Sprenger cherry bellows and Benny McLaughlin wind chimes. Over the years there were hammered dulcimer concerts by Jerry Read Smith; blacksmithing demonstrations by Robert Timberlake of Hillsborough; and Ledbetter and Janet Knight demonstrated bamboo flutes.

In the 1980's he boasted of plans to build the world's tallest pot—and he convinced Mark Hewitt, Michael Sherrill, Brad Tucker, Pam Durgom, Lux and Pat to help him with the feat. He asked customers to bring an hors d'oeuvre in exchange for a coffee mug or $7 off a purchase. Each event had a special, such as $6 coffee mugs for only $4 or maybe 20 percent off wood items. He asked customers to bring desserts to share, and he compiled recipes that he published in a cookbook. He always asked for leftover paper bags and towels and newspapers for wrapping pots, and he always offered door prizes.

He held jack-o-lantern carving contests in the fall and Easter egg hunts in the spring, and the prizes were his crystalline pots, which had become so popular. He invited Charles Zug, the author of "Turners and Burners," to identify pots for customers. In one newsletter, he touted his crystal pots that were "very special this time in that color cannot be repeated." He'd created the soft green-blue glaze by mixing the leftover test glazes together, and he made it sound intentional, when in fact, it had been a fortunate mistake. He announced that customers would be limited to only one of his crystal pots each kiln opening, and that in itself increased demand for his work.

The newsletters revealed some of the pride he felt in his children, announcing when Lisa studied glass in Penland and when she married Craig Chandler. In 2000, a kiln letter praised David and his wife Claire D'Andrea as David began his own advertising business with John Boone. David had become a celebrated creative designer for advertising, winning several Clios and one-show Pencil Awards. His Charlotte Hornets television commercial was voted one of the world's funniest by Comedy Central, and David designed the Alltel ads with Faith Hill. Sid was proud of his children, their spouses and his grandchildren.

He merged his mercantilism with education, and that created consumers who were better informed about the art they appreciated. One form of consumer education came in 1989 when Sid decided to hold a National Teapot Show. He invited craftspeople from all over the country to submit their teapots into a juried show. Manager Bonnie Allen convinced a Tetley Tea representative to attend the show, and he bought a pot.

Sid promoted his gallery as a destination in and of itself, a place to escape the hustle and bustle of the city, an ambiance that had contributed to Seagrove's success. Located in the middle of the state, a trip to Cedar Creek is ideal for a day trip or a weekend away. Sid didn't want to give up what was important to him about his community, the nature and woods, and he wanted to make people slow down and take a look at something.

Other young men and women working at Cedar Creek learned how adept Sid was at working his customers. He'd don his role of the country boy who's done well, and people didn't realize just how much he knew about art— and his customers. Few people saw Sid when he was on the road selling his work or when he was stressed out because of money worries, but those close to him knew he made it look easier than it was. Sometimes Sid's idiosyncrasies resulted in blunders, but he was able to cover them up and move onto something else. Cedar Creek was ultimately his, and he made the final decisions.

Because he was so busy with daily decisions at Cedar Creek, Sid's work was not widely distributed beyond North Carolina. Though he'd made a conscious decision not to form a craft school so that he could create his own work, the daily challenge of running a gallery and marketing work there took most of his time.

Sid has been working daily on his play, and he tells me again that there are people waiting to see it. "I've got to finish it this year, for sure. You can't give it to them until it's finished to your satisfaction." He asks me if I know a tobacco farmer who might recall the auction price for the golden leaf back in the 1950s, and I promise to find a name and number for him and call him back.

He's papered his wrapping station walls with autographed photos of Perry Como, Gregory Peck, Joe Spano, Loretta Lynn and Emmy Lou Harris. He points out that Paul Green wanted to see the play he wrote in 1950, "Dey Calls Me Boo." He received a Christmas card from John Ehle and Rosemary Harris.

I've started to realize just how much Sid appreciates being associated with greatness. In some cases his name-dropping missed the mark with me, because I simply didn't know all the important people's names I ought to know. But he knew how to impress me. In the 1980's, he taught Kaye Gibbons pottery lessons after meeting her as a customer. The two became friends, and she'd join him with white loaf bread, tomatoes, peanuts and RC cola. Together they'd share tomato sandwiches and talk for hours. I actually feel a twinge of jealousy. I know I will stop by the library and check out all her books and reread them. And I'll eat a tomato sandwich for dinner.

Chapter 11

I drove home today struggling with how I was ever going to find Mildred for Sid. My life had become even more disorganized as I tried to record Sid's history, find Mildred and write a few newspaper stories while my children were in school.

I'd told my husband that I was stuck, that I didn't know whom to call to find out about Mildred. He suggested the mayor of Stovall.

"But she's white," I reminded him.

"She knows everyone," he told me, "and she might know who would know."

I dreaded calling another stranger and asking my question. I'd avoided it for as long as I could. I knew that I needed to give enough information to find her, but not enough to scare people from talking to me. It was a delicate balance, one that I'd not yet mastered. I asked it in the most non-threatening way I could. I didn't like to spread rumors, but I felt more and more that I was supposed to find these answers.

My children knew there were times they shouldn't come into my study; they often did anyway. They tried to be unobtrusive by asking "yes" or "no" questions that they knew would be "no" except when I needed them to leave while I was interviewing someone on the phone. I'd say yes to stop them from pantomiming their questions or writing on scraps of paper, so they wouldn't interrupt, which usually distracted me completely from my interview even though they were not actually talking.

When I had a really important phone call, I made my do-not-come-in-here-and-ask-me-anything-while-I-am-on-the-phone speech.

"This is a really important call," I told them. "Do not come in here." I closed the door to the study.

I called the Stovall town hall and spoke with the mayor.

"Do you know anything about a little black girl who was adopted about 60 years ago? Or do you know any old black person who might remember something like that?"

"You might try talking with Hoover," she told me.

I didn't know his first name was James, and that's why I couldn't find his phone number at first. The big black man I knew as Hoover grew up in Stovall, one of eight children that his mother Willie Mae raised by herself. She taught her children to speak to others, and they did, and she taught them to respect others, and they did. Hoover sometimes bought food in the Oxford Café as a young man, but he had to order through the window. He couldn't sit or eat in the drug store. He didn't often have money to spend, but he enjoyed occasional shows at Orpheum Theater, even though he knew he'd have to sit upstairs. He sat behind the sheet that designated the back of the bus, or he stood if the whites filled up the seats.

When we first met, Hoover was a Wal-Mart greeter, and he recognized the irony.

"You know, used to be a time you wouldn't see a black person at a cash register; now that's the most they got," he said as his cat climbed up on the table between us when I'd driven to see him one afternoon.

"Giddown," he said, shoving it gently out of the way.

He recalled a day at an Oxford Fair when he rode to town in his friend's shiny 1957 black Chevrolet. When the two men returned to the car, they found a note on its windshield: "You have been visited by the Knights of the KKK."

"And they wanted us to join because they thought we was white," Hoover chuckled. "I forgot where they said to meet them at."

"People change," he said. "It ain't all gone, and it ain't all the white men. The blacks they've got now, they're just as prejudiced. Some of them blame the children for what their white folks did."

Hoover was the first black man to serve in his town's fire department and the first to serve on his town's council. Whites and blacks worked well together there, he said. His tenure lasted 19 years, and during that time the town built a sewage treatment plant. He's proud of that.

I listened. Quiet seeped under the door from where my children played together. I picked up the phone and dialed Hoover's number. I explained the story again.

"Let me call you back," Hoover said.

I had waited only about 30 minutes, when the phone rang.

"I found your girl," he told me.

Chapter 12

I had the number. Hoover had asked her if I could call, and she'd said yes. Now I needed to dial. My heart thumped; my hands sweated. My husband wasn't home, so he would not be able to stop my children from interrupting me. What would Mildred say when I called to tell her I'd found her because an old white man remembered her from all those years ago? What if she hung up on me?

I stood up and walked back to where my children played a game that they call "guys." An assortment of G.I. Joes stood in army regalia and spy disguises amongst Kate's Barbies dressed in ballet tutus and evening gowns. Kate, Daniel and Michael talked intensely about who was married to whom and who the bad guys were. They were easy to spot since they all happened to be the naked G.I. Joes for whom no clothes could be found.

"You all cannot interrupt me this time," I said in my most serious tone. "This is a really, really important phone call."

"OK, Mom," the youngest three answered in unison, barely looking up from their game. Jack didn't even hear me, engrossed as he was in reading his book.

The dishwasher hummed, the washing machine thumped from a too-large load, the window in the laundry room grew steamy from the dryer's heat escaping from an improperly routed hose. My dogs barked and barked, I stuck my head out to see why, and the goats maaa'd at me. Everything seemed completely normal at my house, so I went back in the study and shut my door.

I sat down by the phone and my new black kitten climbed up my bare leg. I'd named him Luke after rescuing him from beneath our church. Despite my very real claustrophobia, I'd slithered into the crawlspace with a can of wet, smelly cat food to save the starving kitten.

"Get down," I pulled him off my leg and tossed him aside.

I dialed the phone. I asked to speak to Mildred.

"Who's this?" My hearted thumped harder. I said my name, from Oxford, North Carolina.

When that woman handed Mildred the phone, I told my story again, finally to the person who needed to hear it.

"I'm writing a book about a master potter in Granville County," I told her, "but the first time we met he sent me looking for you. He remembers your first day of school. He remembers your yellow dress. He thought it was wrong when it happened to you then, and he's never forgotten you."

"Oh my goodness gracious," she said. She sounded like a New Yorker, like a stereotypical Jewish grandmother. She told me what bits and pieces she recalled.

"I lived with a school teacher and lumber mill owner, and I never wanted for anything," she said. "My father even bought me a brown and white pony."

"What was his name?" I'm writing every detail down.

"Let's see, his name was Pinto," she recalled.

"My people knew where I was," she assured me. "They knew exactly where I was. I'd see a car driving by slowly. Of course they never stopped or anything like that."

She seemed curious about how this had evolved, but harbored none of the bitterness I anticipated, none of the distrust I expected, none of the anger that I felt for her situation. It was almost as if she was hearing a story about someone else; it wouldn't really affect her one way or another. She had another life now in New York.

"To this day I don't care what people say," she told me, and I thought how lucky for her that her mother sent her away when she did. The gumption I heard in her voice I knew she must have inherited from her white mother and refined with her black mother. I wanted to tell her white mother, "You made the right choice." I prayed she knew that before she died.

"Would you mind if I give your number to Sid?" I asked. "I know he'd like to talk with you."

"That's fine," she said.

"Can I call you back in a few days to see if you remember anything else? I know I'm asking you about a time you may not have thought of in years."

"There's really not much to tell."

Luke crawled into my lap, purring loudly. My children stayed out of the room. I sat and thought about Mildred and the gift she'd given me. Her story. I don't know why she talked with me; I'm awed that she did. And in some ways it reinforced my belief that I was right to find her for Sid. Because all along I wasn't sure I should. She'd been wondering about her early years, she told me, but she'd never wanted to find out while her black mother was alive because she didn't want to hurt her.

Mildred had told me that a few days after she was sent home from school, the social workers came in the evening to take her away. She gathered her meager belongings: the three new dresses that her parents had bought her for school and a pair of shoes decorated with little flowers.

The social workers drove 22 miles to her new home with Missouria and James Fain in Stovall in northern Granville County. Only seven miles from the Virginia state line, it seemed like a world away from Stem. I've been told that blacks and whites got along well together in Stovall. The town had grown out of a trading post, Sassafras Fork, which expanded when the railroad passed through it. The town was renamed to honor John Walker Stovall, who donated land for the right-of-way for the Oxford and Clarksville branch of the Southern Railroad, as well as a depot.

Most folks grew their own food and didn't eat out often, but even those who didn't visit the shops knew what went on in them. There was a store that sold hot dogs, and a little place on the corner had chicken sandwiches. Clerks at the drug store scooped ice cream for a nickel a cone; chocolate, strawberry and vanilla, your choice. A customer could try on a new pair of blue jeans or shoes there, too. The meat market held beef wrapped in thick white paper for customers, and another brightly painted store was aptly called "Yellow Store." There was a nightclub in town, and an assortment of churches for the faithful to choose from when they went looking for God.

Several saw mills hummed in town with laborers busy cutting boards to size for any project that happened along. Most of the lumber was oak and pine. There were shoeshine shops, barber shops, and families occasionally stopped near St. Peter's Episcopal Church to enjoy a tent show with vaudeville acts and cowboy movies. It wasn't all that different from downtown Stem in its busyness and businesses. The difference in Stovall, several folks have told me, was that everyone, black and white, went in and out the same door at their neighbors' homes.

The elementary school for black children stood on U.S. Highway 15. It had no indoor bathrooms. That's where Mildred's new mother taught school. Missouria, a fair-skinned black woman, was known for her no-nonsense approach to teaching. Missouria's husband James operated a saw mill, and the couple was considered wealthy.

The social workers walked Mildred up the path to the front door. Missouria opened the door, and James stood next to her. A young boy stood in front of Missouria, studying Mildred on the porch.

"He told me to go back home," Mildred remembered.

Chapter 13

Finally, I call Sid. My heart pounds when I hear his voice.

"I found her. I found Mildred."

I try to tell him everything I know as quickly as I can.

"She lives in New York, and I asked her if you could call her, and she said yes, and here is her number." And then I breathe.

I don't even remember what he said, I was so intent on telling him I'd found her and that he could call her. I wanted him to call her right then.

"She said she'd be up for a while." It's only about 8:30 p.m. I felt that I'd finally done what Sid wanted.

When we meet the following Tuesday, he's already talked to her, and he's made plans to meet her in person. He is back in charge of the situation, taking Mildred out of my hands as easily as he had given me the job of finding her in the first place. I am a little amused. At first I'm not really bothered by it. It is a trait he has, I'd learned. He knew what he wanted done, and when he knew he couldn't do it himself, he found someone who could. But once the obstacle had been overcome, he stepped in to move to the next level of whatever it was that he had planned in the first place. I figured that now I could legitimately work on Sid's story, but I did want to meet her when she came down.

He invited Mildred and her husband to stay with Pat and him on their next trip down to visit her home place in Stovall. I knew by then that this was more than an invitation from Sid. It was meant to show Mildred that part of her white family wanted her back home, even if this particular familial connection was in name only. She had none of his blood in her, but had shared his name until she was seven.

They've already figured out that maybe he met her mother one time years ago when David's teacher Nell Eaton brought another teacher from Stovall out to his shop; such a Southern thing to want to have connections.

Of course, that's what I'd found this story was all about. Connections: intricate and meandering, denied and decried, connections that linked three families in a way that none of them could foresee, and many would have liked to forget. The connections had been destroyed, just as Stem School had been destroyed, just as Sid's home place had fallen into rubble. That amnesia might have been safe if not for Sid, who seemed haunted by the wrong done to Mildred all those years ago

"They're going to sell that property in Stovall," Sid says, because it's too hard to keep an eye on it from such a long distance. He likes knowing what was going on, and he likes for other people to know he knows.

"She told me to call her any time. I promised to take her out where she grew up. It's Mildred who the story's really about."

I nod and say OK, but I think he's just being modest. I'm enthralled with him and the story of how he became what he became. I'm intrigued with Mildred and how she would be willing to talk to me, a stranger calling her out of nowhere, to talk about what likely was the most painful time of her life. Why she would do that, I couldn't understand. But I did know that what she had shown me was real-life grace, more vividly than I could have learned in any Sunday school lesson.

Sid's still going on about their conversation. "She said to me, 'I have been thinking of my early family and what they were like.' "

I didn't tell him that she said the same thing to me, many of the same things she said to him. I wanted him to feel like he knew more than I did. This had been his idea after all. And he looked so thin.

"It certainly did help me because I had this vision, of course, of Mildred in that chair, not knowing what happened to her, and now I know that she did leave there and do well."

"It's like I told Mildred on the phone, 'well, there are good people and there are bad people everywhere.'

"Right away she said, 'Yes, there are.' "

I knew Sid felt frustrated because those whom he had called in Mildred's family didn't want to meet her. He liked to make things happen, and this was out of his control. It didn't appear that it would have the happy ending he envisioned. Instead, Mildred could be hurt again. I didn't know how he would pull it off, but somehow I expected him to work his magic to reunite this family. It would be a challenge because the shame of the incident still haunted the white relatives, though none of the main characters in the story was still alive.

"I think their children and grandchildren don't know anything about this," Sid speculates. "Mildred's family, they see it as a scandal. There's some very positive things that their grandchildren would be proud of. Their mother accepted this child as their own, their father did, too. Eventually some time or another they're going to find out about it."

For Sid, this was a picture not yet complete, and he was determined to put his final brushstrokes on her story. I worried about the ending because I know that art makes you feel, but it doesn't always make you feel good.

We talk a little more about how we might find Mildred's father, and Sid plans to make a few calls. I will research other leads at the library. We agree we need to find her father to complete her story.

"You know you could write this as fiction. You don't even have to do it right now. It could be 10 years from now. You have the sensitivity to do this."

I don't tell him that I'm afraid to try.

Chapter 14

The quince paint cherry-colored brushstrokes among the newly greening spring. I peer through the window above the table and see Sid's daughter Lisa's glass studio, just 60 steps from the main gallery. Daffodils push the leaf litter aside, dotting the neutral browns and tans with brilliant yellow and orange.

First we talk about his plans for Mildred's visit.

"If she comes down maybe me and you and Dudley and Pat could go out to eat with Mildred and Bill." He mentions a local restaurant.

"They give you a lot of food, and it's good."

Though he's told me he was never hungry as a child, I sometimes find that hard to believe because so many of his memories include food: boyhood fishing games that resulted in piles of fish, pizza in Germany and pork chop biscuits in town. Quantity always seems to be a consideration in the evaluation of the culinary experience.

Today, Sid gives me two boxes of paper clips. I thank him, even as I wonder if he finds me totally disorganized.

"These are the best paper clips," he assures me. I smile to myself as I consider how one paper clip could be better than another and why it mattered.

Some are rainbows of plastic, some only gray stainless steel. Some are big, some are small. Some have textures, others don't. Some can't hold many papers, but are ideal for gripping two or three sheets together, though they'd stretch to busting if you tried to bundle more than eight pages. Some leave imprints on the front and back pages, rusting over time. Others don't grip tightly enough to hold anything together for any time at all. But they all share a common purpose: to establish connections and groups among separate pieces.

I tell Sid that I'm frustrated because my second son has just learned that his best little girlfriend is black. It happened in kindergarten, almost overnight. I don't know who told him that he can't marry Javona because she is black. I'm so sad.

"I don't understand," he says. "There are black people I don't like to associate with; there are a lot of white people I don't like to associate with, but it's not based on color."

"I'm a lot more open to people. Sometimes I see people from Stem, and they assume I think like them. I just think differently from them. It was the more educated and mercantile class that were so prejudiced. The common poor were not."

When David started kindergarten in 1967, schools were not integrated, but David was assigned to a black teacher named Nell Eaton. She loved David, who loved her right back. Sid told her one day, "If anyone gives you any trouble, you call me. I think you're a great teacher. I want you to teach my son."

Although David heard what he calls "the 'N' word" all the time at school and in the community, his parents taught him everyone was the same. He asked his father why people were called "nigger."

"The people who say that are ignorant," Sid told his son. "You do not use that word. It's not respectful. To be honest, David, I had more in common with black people growing up than white people who had a lot of money."

Linwood Harris and Sid have been friends for years since the black contractor built the Oakley's shop at Cedar Creek. He's restored old tobacco barns for Sid and taken adventurous trips with him. For example, in Biloxi, Mississippi, they made $6,000 on slot machines.

"He's got the fever," Harris smiles. They're planning a trip to Atlantic City together. He sits on his back porch beneath the most beautiful shade tree I've ever seen. It feels like we're sitting in air-conditioning, protected by the big boughs that my son would love to climb.

"I can tell that tree anything," he says.

Harris sips from his coffee cup. He grew up in Creedmoor, which he never found to be too prejudiced. In the late 1950's, the town children had snowball fights: blacks against the whites. They shot basketball together on Main Street and visited each other's homes, sharing meals together. His children grew up with Sid's and Pat's children, swimming in the pool with them and attending birthdays and Christmas parties. He tells me Sid is a die-hard democrat, "a democrat from his heart," who hates prejudice and loves jazz.

One of their ongoing dialogs centers on Sid's funeral plans. Several years back, Harris had stopped by Cedar Creek and Sid asked him to be a pallbearer at his funeral, which he was planning at the time. A couple years later, Sid told him he'd had a change of plans.

"Linwood, I've decided to be cremated, so I won't need you as a pallbearer," Sid told him. But the next year, Sid announced to Harris that he might need his help after all because he'd decided to be buried again.

"You're not born prejudiced," Harris said. "You see white kids three and four years old, they go out and they play together, but later on it's another thing. I treat them the way they treat me. You can spot a person who's prejudiced. You can see it before you even have any dealings with that person. My Mom and Dad taught me everybody's somebody."

When he was a child, Sid had asked his mother about the Klan.

"My mother told me it was secret and mean, that's all she told me," he said. As recently as the 1970's, U.S. Highway 15 held a sign with the words, "The KKK welcomes you to Granville County." When Sid saw the Klan sign on the highway, he thought, "Well, she probably knew what she was talking about."

Sid knew Klan members came from all walks of life and ascended into all levels of government and law enforcement. For many folks, separating blacks and whites was what they grew up knowing. Blacks and whites drank from different fountains; they attended different schools; they worshipped in different churches.

Sid's seen many changes in his lifetime in how people feel and how they act.

"I remember in 1956 when Luther Hodges, who was governor, urged voluntary segregation of the races in schools," he recalls. "In the Air Force we had this incredible black basketball player...I thought, 'If you could go to Carolina that would be great.' Of course, he couldn't at that time.

"I have seen local people change. I remember when they integrated the cafeteria in Butner. In the early sixties all the white people sat on one side. Now everybody sits together. It's different now."

A few years back, Sid asked Harris, "What do you think of George Wallace?"

"He told me, 'The man got up and said he was sorry, he was wrong for what he did. When a man stands up and says he's sorry, you forgive him.'

"I think black people have a way of forgiving that white people don't have," Sid says. After the Department of Defense pulled out its troops, Butner faced a daunting task, but also a unique opportunity. It became a town full of firsts. It held the first Alcoholic Rehabilitation Center, the first School for the

Blind, the inaugural First Offender program. At John Umstead Hospital, many of the doctors were refugees from World War II. It was and is the only town run by the state, giving it an opportunity to lead integration because of its unique composition and organization.

Frank Askins was chaplain at Umstead Hospital during its early years of conversion from a barracks to a state institution. At one time the hospital held 2,100 patients, with the locals providing the hands-on care.

Twice a Sunday, Askins led services there in a packed auditorium, and he also provided pastoral counseling. He and Sid crossed paths in their different roles at the different institutions, and soon found they shared common interests. In 1957 Askins began raising bees, which fascinated Sid, and he started a few hives of his own. He promises to give me the old preformed plastic comb that he still has in a shed somewhere because I, too, have begun a bee hive.

Butner's organization also made it unusual because in the state-run town, there were no community activities. In the late 1950's, Sid decided there ought to be something for the youth to do: Little League baseball. Askins's boys were prime ball-playing age, and he and his wife Ruth supported Sid's plan.

"He was a visionary," Askins said. "He was the right man at the right place at the right time. Sid was the yeast and salt of the Old Testament."

But once they began talking about the league, they realized there was no town manager or town government to ask about starting it. Sid approached all the department heads of the institutions to pitch his idea for the youth league, and everyone told him, "You can't do that."

Next, Sid organized a public meeting in a Sunday school room at Butner Baptist Church. Many folks attended, and a couple of people donated $25, which purchased the equipment the first year. The ball games became successful, with locals contributing wild game they'd hunted to make big batches of Brunswick stew, fundraisers that paid for the uniforms the first summer.

It wasn't long before the ball club became integrated because organizers saw no reason to exclude boys because of their race.

Chapter 15

When Lisa came to work today, she heard bagpipes blaring "Amazing Grace" coming from her parents' window open to the fall air. She cried.

Sid, however, was happy that he'd finally found the version of the classic Christian song that he'd been searching for. Though he's been planning his funeral for years, now he seems more focused, and he's looking for songs to put on his funeral tape. He wants people to tell a few jokes. It's ironic in a way that he plans to include the most traditional of all funeral songs in his clearly non-traditional approach.

Sid had a broader interpretation of God. The order in nature had convinced him of a Supreme Being.

"I really think painting and making pottery is some kind of religious experience in itself," he says. "The creating, when you're creating something, it's a very positive thing, and you can't separate it. You can't separate your writing from religion or making pots from religion or painting from religion. All that stuff comes together to make a whole it creates.

"I know that God would look down and smile on you and me when we have done something well," Sid says.

"Or he might say, 'Try harder next time,'" I add, and we laugh.

I had a dilemma, and I wanted his opinion. The largest newspaper in our area had called with a faith story for me to write. I was so excited I said, "Sure, I'd love to do it." But that was before I'd asked what the story was about. It was about atheists, how they were all around us, and the story would make them human and understandable and sympathetic at a time when everyone was riled up about the debate over taking "under God" out of the Pledge of Allegiance.

I knew some Christians would think badly of me if I did it. But I really wanted to write for this paper. And in my own mind, I'd become less judgmental toward people who didn't share my beliefs. In some cases, I realized, I didn't always know what's right. I had doubts, too. I knew I shouldn't care what everyone thinks.

"Sid, do you think God did this to test me?"

"No," he says. "God would not do that."

"I believe very, very strongly in the power of prayer myself," he explains. "I am not that much on organized religion because I don't know if it's all that close to what Jesus was talking about. They do a lot of good, and for a lot of people it's very good, and so I respect it, and we should have it, but it's not for me."

He told me his friend married a woman who spoke in tongues, and the Christian couple cast out their blind son because they claimed he was "afflicted."

"I said 'what kind of damn religion do you have that tells you to treat your own son like that?' And then he quoted Scripture to justify casting him out."

"Drinking was out. I'd say, 'If Jesus was to walk in here today, he would choose to go and sit with me in a hot tub and drink a beer and talk. He would want to do that. He wouldn't want you to wash his feet.' That was just blasphemy."

With the beginning of their family, Sid and Pat had looked for a church where they could establish a spiritual foundation.

Presbyterian minister Al Thomas had come to Butner to organize a new church in 1957. He'd grown up on a farm and worked nights at a textile mill, so he could attend Davidson College. In his first church in Johnston County, he'd been invited to a community meeting to figure out a way to get around the new integration laws. When he didn't attend, those same community leaders burned a cross in his yard.

Butner was unusual because it held so many state institutions, which housed both blacks and whites. The residents in those programs had no vehicles, so if they wanted to go somewhere, they walked. When Thomas's church was built in 1958, its location made it an easy walk from several institutions. Those who lived and worked in Butner institutions were often well-educated, and as a result, his church members included psychiatrists, social workers, nurses and doctors.

Black people joined white people in worship at Thomas's church, and Sid appreciated that openness. Sid's extended family's early faith foundations were Primitive Baptist, which do have some roots akin to Presbyterians. Both share a strong sense of the sovereignty of God.

"He had a strong faith, but he had a lot of problems with the institutional church," Thomas recalled. Sid preferred his role as an iconoclast.

Nevertheless, Sid was baptized in 1963 and later served as a deacon at the church, and Thomas shows me the papers that recorded the events.

After his father died, Sid's Aunt Lessie, who was his father's sister, came and stayed with the family for a week.

"She was very, very, very religious, some strange religion," Sid says.

"She wouldn't even drink Pepsi Cola, but she would drink True Ade. It didn't have any carbonated water in it. I thought, 'My God, what has that got to do with it?' I didn't like her. I thought, 'What has that got to do with church?'"

"I liked her a lot the last 10 years that I knew her. She wasn't as religious as I'd perhaps thought she was."

Although some of Sid's extended family's faith was rooted in the Primitive Baptist tradition, his immediate family didn't attend formal services anywhere very often. But there was one church event that Sid attended religiously: Vacation Bible School at Geneva Presbyterian Church. His faithfulness stemmed not from a particular belief, but from his passion for banana sandwiches.

Geneva Church always scheduled Bible School for the week of July 4 because that was when tobacco was laid by. Farmers had already cultivated, planted and weeded, and that week was set aside for waiting for the plants to grow—and for Vacation Bible School. Local church-going farmers hooked their farm trailers to their trucks and drove around the neighboring farm roads picking up the children for Bible School.

After a week full of Bible learning for both adults and children, Bible School concluded on Saturday with a covered dish supper. And just as fried chicken remains a staple on church tables today, in those days suppers always had banana sandwiches.

"Before they said the prayer," Sid confesses, "I would look around the table and find out where they were and stand right in front of them. 'Cause that's the only time of the year I had a banana sandwich. I know if it wasn't for those banana sandwiches I wouldn't have gone."

That's when I told him my secret. When I was 16, I wanted to become Jewish.

I'd just read James Michener's *The Source*. I read of the deep, deep beginnings of faith, then I read of the persecution of the Jewish people. By Christians. I hated the Christians for that. But I didn't know how I could become Jewish and reject everything I'd been taught since before I could speak. I'm Methodist, and my parents promised they'd raise me in the church, and they did.

I've never doubted there's Someone up there greater than me. I've felt a close connection with Him, and I talked to Him all the time. It probably wasn't the right way to talk to God. I thanked Him for the indigo bunting in my yard. I thanked Him for my children. I prayed that He'd watch over my best friend as she cared for her sister with schizophrenia. I thanked Him for letting me not get a rejection letter today in the mail, even though that's a reverse double negative or something.

It was grace that I couldn't comprehend. I couldn't understand that saying "I accept Jesus as my Lord and Savior" would get me to heaven. No matter what horrible things I've done, no matter whom I've hurt. No matter my sins, which I'm not going to confess. There's His grace. And all I have to do is accept it.

That sounded too easy. I knew better than that. There was a certain amount of suffering that must be done for any particular sin. I learned that, too.

I could relate to God in the Old Testament, in most cases. I understood the vindictive punishments that He doled out to those who didn't do as He said. I struggled with His command for Abraham to kill his own son, just to see if He'd do it. I hated that story, too. I would never be able to prove my faith by something like that.

For some reason, Jack would always turn to that story in his Big Golden Bible. I'd try to redirect him. He was only two. But that's the story Jack wanted me to read over and over and over again. He turned to it every time. So I changed what it said; he couldn't read, after all.

"God didn't really want him to kill his son, and Abraham wasn't really going to do it," I'd explain to my child. "God just wanted to see if he would to see how much he loved Him."

I felt God had used my children to remind me He is here. During a visit to a friend's house when Michael was four, he peered up at the skylight and asked, "Is that how God sees inside your house?" On a spring-like day, he yelled at the top of his lungs, "Thank you, God."

One typical evening, we asked Jack, Michael and Daniel to clean up their room, Kate's room and the den, and then they would be able to watch a short video. Michael had always been a hard worker, and he approached the task with his usual determination. And then I heard him singing. A song none of us had ever heard before. To a tune, that, well, it was a tune of some sort.

His song went like this: "I think the Lord is great." Thump, as he tossed the Fisher-Price garage in Kate's closet.

"God bless God. God bless sticks. God bless everything that You made." Bang, bang, bang went several toys as he tossed them into the plastic bin.

"And it's wonderful. God bless God. He is a nice Man." Crash went the play radio that started to play "London Bridge is falling down."

"It's my God. I like God. I am His friend."

Michael's God made sticks, he made our days, and he peered in our skylights at night, and I knew Him, too.

Sid pauses between breaths. His lips tighten, and he looks angry. He must think about each breath he breathes. When I see it and think it, I take a deep breath because I feel my own chest tighten. Sid and I only talk briefly this afternoon. It is hot, and I am sweaty. He wears a flannel shirt, his shoes unlaced because his feet have swelled. I hand him the first rough draft of my work.

It is not ready to be read. It's just that I worried he might think I wasn't really writing all his information down. I thought he might think I was just coming to listen to his stories, much like I did with my Grandma Selma. And if he thought that, he'd be partly right. I loved his voice, its cadence and language and pauses. I loved his thoughts and memories as he remembered and created them. Because I was not a part of his past, I could listen without fear of hearing something that might hurt me. I wanted to be truthful as I documented his life, and I trusted Sid would tell me the truth. I realized later that Sid told me his truth, whether the facts supported it or not.

Sid reads the first five paragraphs.

"This is great. I can't wait to read it all. I'm going to sit right here and read it right now."

It's time for me to pick up my daughter from preschool, but as I stand to leave, Sid stops me. The last thing he tells me today is that he met a black angel. Sid was returning to Cedar Creek in a new van he and Pat had purchased. He'd stood in the dealership as the salesperson told him all the directions for the car, where all the important papers were and how to unlock the tire-changing paraphernalia, but he admits he hadn't paid a bit of attention. Pat drove their old car home, and Sid followed her in the new van.

"Sure enough I had a flat tire," he laughs. "I don't have a clue. I thought, 'what am I going to do? I'll just sit here until Pat misses me.' " He waited 15 minutes.

"I met a real angel. He didn't have wings, but I know he was an angel. Here was this black man running toward me as fast as he could, toward me from down at the service station. 'It looks like you need some help. I'm going to help you. People give to my father all the time. This is one way I can give back.'"

"Wasn't that nice of him?" Sid asks.

I worry that it's a premonition of something I cannot bear to consider, but Sid assures me that it's been several years.

"He was an angel. I know he was."

As I drive away, I wonder if he thinks I'm capturing his story accurately. I worry that he won't like some of what he's said. Some of the stories seem so personal, I worry he might edit them out. I never allow anyone to read what I write before it's published, unless my source and I speak different languages, and I want to make sure I understood everything correctly. In those cases, I just want them to check the facts. That's what I want Sid to do, to see if I had the story in the right order. To check the facts.

I hear nothing from him for five days. Finally, I call to see when I can meet with him again. My heart pounds as I ask what he thought.

"I liked the first part, but the rest didn't hold up. All you did was string a bunch of quotes together."

I cannot talk. My throat shut, and I'm glad I'm on the phone so he can't see me cry. I can barely ask, "So can we meet next Tuesday at 11 a.m.?"

He says "fine," and we say good-bye.

Chapter 16

"Do you like kiwis?" he asks me. "Here, take you some."

The kiwis come from a vine left to Sid by an 81-year-old woman he met one day at the shop. He only knew her the last four years of her life. Last year, the vine produced 3,000 kiwis.

"They're high in vitamin C. You can store them in the refrigerator for months, and they'll keep."

The woman I came to call "the kiwi lady" drove a little green Volkswagen and bought 12 bluebird houses. A few miles away, she built a 9,000-square-foot house with only one bedroom. The house also held a grooming room for her beagles, a file room and a canning room.

"I was the first person to eat at her house in over 20 years," Sid says. "I didn't know she had any money. We would talk. When her husband died, she took him and buried him, then called her kids."

When the kiwi lady learned she had cancer, she asked Sid if she should take chemotherapy.

"I couldn't tell her yes or no. Looking back I would have said no."

He seems to be moving slower, talking less.

I ask Sid for more details about the maypops, the flower that he drew for his Mayflower assignment.

"It's a passion flower," Sid says. "It has that fruit on it, you possibly could eat that fruit, it was real good if you let it stay on until the frost came."

The blooms combine vibrant reds and pinks right next to each other on the same plant, Sid explains.

He won't tell me the name of his teacher who told him he had no talent. His view of her has softened with age.

Over the years, Sid continued to hire the LeSueurs to perform at his kiln openings.

"Come sit down," he said one evening after they'd played all day. "I've been thinking about this, and I really think you ought to make a CD, and I will back you. I like your music, and I think it's important.

"I also think you need to charge more for your performances, and from now on I'm paying you more. And here's an early Christmas bonus."

Though they felt they couldn't accept his offer, they began pondering the possibility of making a CD themselves. They valued his opinion. A few years later they produced "Live at the Little River." Whenever the LeSueurs performed, Sid would stop by and note, "This is our best day we've ever had." They just laughed because he told them that whenever they played.

"I'm ready for my song," he'd say. Number five, "The Last Thing on My Mind." He would punch it over and over and over again while he was throwing pots. After they played it, he'd wander away. Pattie knew he was hiding out, and she'd look for him so they could share a smoke.

"I'm so damn tired of smiling," he told her.

Up until she died, Sid had remained close to his mother, regularly bringing her flowers or taking her with him to the local Farmer's Market where they would buy seeds for her garden. He took her to lunch often.

His sister Hallie lived in Butner, and Sid and Pat invited her on family trips to Florida, where she'd watch the children while they looked at the work of other craftspeople at the craft fairs. If Hallie mentioned a pretty rose she'd seen in a catalog, it wouldn't be long before she'd find it at her house. She tried to pay him, but Sid would tell her, "That'll be a banana pudding" or maybe two or three banana puddings. She used a recipe from Southern Living, and once he even charged her five banana puddings, but she can't remember why.

In December 2003, Ben Owen III visited Sid and took him a Chinese blue pot he'd made. Sid was excited, and the two began talking. Sid began showing some pots and things from years past, talking about copper red glazes, giving Owen pointers as they discussed pots that were sitting around the house.

"That's a beautiful bowl, Sid," Owen said.

"Here, take it home with you," Sid answered.

"Sid, don't do that," Owen protested. "I appreciate you offering."

But then Ben thought back to his time studying in Japan when he had learned about proper gift etiquette. In Japan, when a person gives a gift, he does it because it brings him joy. He took the bowl and added, "Thank you, Sid. It's beautiful."

When I ask Sid what he considers to be his greatest accomplishment, he again surprises me.

"The most important thing to me is being a husband and father and the other things kind of pale. I would like for Pat and the kids to think of me and say, 'Well, he was a pretty decent person.'

"Your best one would be that your kids think of you and smile."

Sometimes during the day you can hear him talking in the background, explaining how to remove air bubbles by wedging a chunk of clay. But that's just a video, taped years ago. At first it sounds natural hearing his voice again where it should be, amid his paintings and pots, his Matisse books and metal lunch boxes, his candied orange slices and cigarettes. He's not in the gallery so often now, and it isn't until later that I learn just how hard it has been for him to meet with me for our weekly talks.

He joked with Lisa in his typical irreverent fashion that, "My disease is CCD--Camels and clay dust."

When Lisa talks about her father, she calls him Daddy first, then Sid in the next breath. It's a conversational convention that she and David developed while working as youngsters in the gallery. They didn't want to call out "Mom" and "Dad" while waiting on customers and appear to be the children that they were. It's just one example of how hard it has been to separate a family business from family.

Knowing Sid was nearby gave Lisa reassurance about the decisions she made in her role as director of the gallery, which Sid has handed over to her several times in recent years. When someone dials the phone from another office while she's trying to talk, sending seven beeps loudly into her ear, she laughs, "Sid used to do that all the time."

The art community in the surrounding area recognizes that his impact extended beyond his work. By carrying high-quality work from a variety of craftspeople, he helped customers learn what they liked and why they liked it. By featuring craftspeople at work, Sid fostered an intimacy among the artists and their customers that often created long-time relationships.

In his nearby studio, Tucker sits at his wheel, covered in stoneware slip, throwing large traditional, functional vases that Sid loved. The two sat together at least for some time every single day. He says that because Sid's vision was kind of odd, he felt compelled to follow it. Sid had his "idears" and he was adept at talking with the public and the press.

As Sid steps back from his daily duties in the shop, among the family there has been no infighting or power struggle: Lisa prefers to be the creative spirit; Pat owns and operates Therapeutic Bodywork; David's busy with his own company, Boone/Oakley Advertising in Charlotte.

When Sid's family realized just how sick he was, David called a family meeting, and they asked him where he wanted Cedar Creek to go.

"I think you guys, whatever direction you feel like it needs to take, that's the direction it needs to take," Sid said. They were frustrated. He knew then, though, that with those words, he was giving them the freedom they would need to move forward.

When Sid acted as contractor for Lisa's glass blowing studio, situated just up the hill from the gallery, he dug up an old rock step to one of the outbuildings. He built a bench with the rock, and he said all of his ancestors had sat on it. A granddaddy long legs hangs underneath the greenish gray seat, worn smooth over the years, a space just right for two placed between their two studios.

Lisa told him, "'I'm going to sit on that rock bench when I need you.'

And Sid said, 'I'll be there.'"

His confrontation of his mortality has made me more aware of my own aging. He assures me that bifocals will be easy to adjust to when I explain how I can no longer read fine print. Next, I confess to him that my husband and I had never named a guardian for our four children. My husband and I differed in our approach to this topic, as we differed on many topics. I wanted to decide who would be the best people to care for our children, to raise them to be empathetic, responsible, happy people. He trusted that someone would do the right thing without some commitment prior to our demise. I didn't trust like that, and my tendency to want to control the future or at least give it a shove in the right direction took over.

This is not to say I hadn't thought about whom to ask. My problem was that for each family I had considered, I found a problem. Families were too old, or one person drank too much or yelled too much or watched too much television or had too much money or too little money or pushed the children too hard or didn't push them hard enough. Other families would probably take one or two but not all four. Whoever did this must take all four. I finally realized that the reason I couldn't decide whom to ask was because each family had a critical flaw: it wasn't my husband and me. At one point, I thought I knew whom to ask, but I wanted to talk it over first with the family.

"Don't do it," my husband said. "If you do this, it will be really weird and then you'll think they're waiting for you to die to get your children. Don't ask. Just write it down and make sure our accountant knows where the document is.'"

"And if I die, I've already thought I need to write a will about where my animals go," I said to him. "You're not going to want to keep all the goats, but you have to make sure Magic has a good home. What makes me mad is that you have such a positive attitude about this, I know you'll remarry and be just fine."

He burst out laughing. "I'd be lost without you."

Of course, whenever I did this, I intended to include a list of directions.

"Teach my children to value a blooming tulip and a baby rabbit. Help them understand that hitting a home run is great, but striking out is OK too. Make sure that they know school is important, but making the best grade isn't the most important thing. Take them to church and nurture their faith. Make sure they know that what they do matters—from picking up trash to listening to a friend. Let them play in the dirt and ride horses and pet goats and save snakes and squirrels. Help them to learn how to be happy. And my most important commandment: Love my children, and make sure they know it."

"Well, write it down, and you can always change it," Sid says.

"But what if I die before I can change it?" I laugh, but I'm not joking.

"Well, that's better than not doing it."

"Do you think it's a silly idea to write my own funeral?" he asks me.

"No," I tell him. "I would expect something unusual from you. But I really wish you would stop talking about it."

"I just want to do it, and get it through and put it in a safe deposit box and go on from there. It won't take me but one day to do it. That's what I was looking for that CD for."

"I've smoked way too many cigarettes in my life."

"I'd like you to talk at my funeral. I hope you don't move too far away any time soon."

I didn't really know what to say. Of course I'd do it. I didn't want to think of it. And I'd come back from wherever I was to do just about anything Sid asked me. I reassured myself that he'd simply started up that old funeral talk with me as he had in the past with Harris; that this would be a long time away. We wouldn't be moving any time soon. In my subconscious I recognize the truth, but we keep meeting and talking. He talks of Hospice, and I feel a sense of terror.

"Did you know that Hospice will help with regular health type problems?" he tells me. "It doesn't always have to be end-of-life needs." I choose to believe him.

"I am getting better because I've been through hell the last three months. I never prepared to get old. I just never thought I would. I never thought I'd have anything wrong with me. I just never prepared for that."

On his funeral tape, Sid will announce, "I decided since this was my day, I would have a non-traditional type funeral."

To Pat he will say, "I love you, I thank you for being by my side all these many years....You sort of made me what I have been."

We were at a stopping point. I packed up my papers to leave, and that's when Sid said something I'd never have expected. He looked grayer. I'm worried about him.

"I think we'd better just let Mildred look for her family. I got the feeling her husband Bill wanted to be the one to find out what happened, so I think you'd better just drop it."

Tonight I call Mildred. She's friendly, as she has been every time we've talked. We talk about Sid and how amazing it is that he would have remembered her after all these years. I always feel a little awkward talking with her. I supposed it was her grace again, and I doubted that I'd ever be comfortable with it.

"It doesn't matter to me," she declares. "I don't mind at all if you try to find out. You're only telling the truth."

"So do you know when you'll be coming down?" I ask.

"In a month or so," she replies.

"Good," I say. "Sid's beach trip is before that, but he'll be back home by then."

Sid doesn't like to talk about his health, and I don't feel it is my place to share his situation. I had to stop myself from saying, "Hurry."

Instead I say, "That's great. I can't wait for you to meet Sid."

Chapter 17

I know she's already arrived at Cedar Creek, and she's met Sid and Pat. I wonder what they're talking about, and I wonder how she feels. I grab a yellow notepad and my tape recorder as my husband and I head out the door for dinner.

When we walk into Sid's house, Mildred is sitting on the couch with Sid. Her husband Bill stands near the kitchen counter talking with Pat.

Mildred is as light-skinned as me. Very pretty. And she talks quick like the New Yorker she is. She reminds me of an olive-skinned Italian grandmother, but I know that's a stereotype. I feel like I shouldn't be here. It seems a stage set with the key characters ready to perform, but there's no script. In some ways I want to disappear, but more than that, I want to hear what they say, to write it and to remember it.

"I was really nervous right before they got here," Sid tells us all. He hasn't shaved. He's sitting sunken into the couch.

I hand her two birth certificates that I've found, proof of her two lives.

It's a little awkward standing there. An expectancy in the air. If Mildred felt uncomfortable, she didn't show it. She's dainty like a little bird, perched on the edge of the couch next to Sid, discussing the drive down to Creedmoor and how she vaguely remembers a trip to this part of the county with her mother.

Sid explains that we won't be eating where he'd originally planned because he felt their last meal there hadn't been up to standards.

Instead, we leave for Another Thyme, a restaurant in Durham, and I cannot help but wonder if Sid intended the metaphor.

We drive our own car and follow the four of them about 20 miles to the restaurant. I debate whether to take a notebook into the restaurant or not. Instead, I tear off a few sheets of yellow paper and fold them into my purse with a pen. Thyme droops over the brick planter that edges the restaurant.

White Christmas tree lights intertwined among the grapevines dimly light the room. It's hard to hear because of the music. This probably isn't the place to ask Mildred to recount all the details of her life. Memories shared over a glass of wine and an elegant dinner.

Above the bar, glowing bottles of spirits stand in all sorts of shapes and colors: long tall goldens and short rich reds, bulbous blues. A battered brick wall adorns the far side of the restaurant, and peach-colored roses top each table. We're sitting in a booth, and a horizontal series of beach prints hangs in a frame between us. Mildred, Sid and Bill sit across from Pat, my husband and me. I feel like I shouldn't be here, yet I feel like I'm supposed to be here. Sid seems quiet tonight.

Mildred fell in love with New York from the moment she arrived. She loved working there, the excitement of people having to "go to the floor," with performers in the streets during lunch. She loved the energy.

Although she believes relationships between blacks and whites have improved, she still notices racism in her everyday life.

"There's racist people everywhere," she said. "I don't know when it's going to stop."

The waitress walks up to our table, and it's time to order.

"Order anything you like," Sid commands.

I have a salad; my husband finally decides on an expensive steak, and that makes Sid happy. Mildred orders some kind of fish. Sid picks chicken. Pat chooses tilapia, and Bill orders a pork chop, which Sid assures him will be delicious.

When we finish our meal, Sid disappears. It takes a few moments before anyone comments on his escape.

"He's probably out smoking," Pat says.

"Oh, he needs to stop," Mildred says. "I stopped the day I went to the doctor, and he told me how bad my lung capacity was. I came home and smoked my last two cigarettes, and that was that."

It's clear to all of us just how hard it is for Sid to breathe. It's also clear to all of us he won't stop smoking. We all know that it probably isn't worth trying to stop him now.

"He needs to get a nebulizer," Mildred says. "That helped me. I could breathe so much better. Does he use oxygen at all?"

Pat says no.

"You need to get his doctor to prescribe these," Mildred says. "I can't believe they haven't already given this to him. It's not that hard to use. It makes such a difference."

I hope Pat will be able to convince Sid to try these ideas.

My husband leaves the table to find Sid. He tells him we're all plotting how to make him stop smoking, and Sid laughs. We agree to meet in the morning at Cedar Creek. Sid is going to take Mildred home.

Chapter 18

The next morning wakes gray, washed out and nearly colorless. Sid sits in the front seat with Bill. Mildred and Pat are in the back. Smooth jazz rumbles from the rental car's radio as the four prepare to revisit where Mildred was born. They share bits of their own histories as they drive down the back roads of Creedmoor, on their way to the crossroads known as Stem.

Mildred studies a local history of Stem in the back seat.

"Turn right," Sid says. "Turn left here."

"People talk too damn much, that's true," Mildred states.

Though Mildred knew she was adopted, she didn't realize there was a trail to follow. "I have two birth certificates now," she says. "I knew I was adopted because I was six years old. Those things have a way of surfacing one way or another. If it's nothing but an old family friend, somebody's going to say something."

We drive in silence for a few moments. I don't know what I expect to happen. I believe Sid needs to show her what he can to validate her beginnings, to show her where she came from. If not for Mildred, then for his own peace of mind.

She doesn't seem nearly as bothered by all this as Sid and I are. She does seem curious, and she does seem to appreciate that Sid cared enough to remember her. But it's almost as if she's watching an old movie about someone else with her same name, interested in what she might recognize but not expecting anything.

"We're coming into Stem now," Sid announces. "This is a little town called Stem. There's always been four to five little stores here that catered to the farmers."

"Stem Town Hall," Mildred notes as she passes a little white house, then a green sign directing drivers to a nearby crossroads. "Tally Ho--oh my gosh."

Providence, Shoofly, Enon, Shiloh, Gela. Reciting the names of the crossroads in Granville County reminds me of my childhood, reading Beatrix Potter's simple, perfect words covering the squeaky pages in the small green books.

"Right there used to be a store on the left and that's where we did all of our trading. That was where Jean Washington's father had a store."

"You might stop for just a minute," Sid says to Bill. "Right beside the home economics building, that's where you came to school that morning. This out here, people played softball in the yard. As you can see by these buildings, it was a pretty nice school. Why they tore it down, I do not know."

Mildred remembers that a black family lived near her house, and she used to play there.

I imagine that deep down, she must have known. She must have known all along that something was different, even with no one telling her. Maybe her black neighbors were kinder to her. Maybe she felt unspoken judgments from her relatives. Maybe she felt whisperings brushing her back as she pressed her pink palm into her white daddy's scratchy hand.

We drive a little farther, listening to the radio.

"You came down this road and turned here," Sid tells Mildred. "This was not a paved road here."

Mildred doesn't seem bitter at all. Just curious. Like she's reading an interesting book and hopes to learn something along the way. She seems to have escaped the pain that I still feel when I think about what happened to her.

"Drive slow. Wait a minute, we're coming to it. OK. Stop right here.

"This is where you got off the school bus, Mildred. Right there."

We really can't see anything except a few trees and new houses.

"Now that house up there was not there, the one behind you. Sitting way up there, it's sort of cleared up now. This used to go on down there. Drive on just a little bit, turn left. Way back in the woods, that's Mildred's house. It's way back in the woods."

Sid directs Bill to head down another road and approach the spot from another direction, hoping something will be there that Mildred will recognize.

"You came right up here and went straight down there. I'm going to try to get in there another way. That's where you walked from down there, all the way up here."

"I know there was a path through the woods," Mildred peers out the window.

"Yeah, this used to be woods here," Sid explains. "But that's where you spent your first six years."

This is it. What I've been waiting for. I don't know if Mildred has, but I think Sid has. He wants closure, even if it's only pointing through the woods to a path covered in brush and weeds that leads to a worn-out house that we can't see.

"All this was trees here, just a little pathway through here. This may be that trailer park. This road wasn't here. If I'm not mistaken, see, none of this was here. You came through these woods over yonder and walked here and came back down this way. That was a long walk."

"Yes, it was," Mildred states.

"Do you remember what your mother said?" Sid asks.

"No, I really don't. I remember I told them they don't want me to go to school, what they said. I remember I was crying, you know."

An ancient oak tree the diameter of a pickup tire still stands, now shading the weeds.

"I think your house was situated down here," Sid continues. "I see that old big tree right here. That would have been there. But I think this is pretty much it."

Most of the past has decayed or disappeared in overgrowth, silently returning to the rich earth. We drive past the school again and pass the cemetery. We're going in circles.

"Your mother, she had a sister named Mildred, so you were named after your aunt," Sid says. "Dr. Thomas delivered you."

"He delivered me, too," Pat adds. Another connection, however strained.

"I don't understand why you aren't bitter," I say, as I've said to many black people during this journey for Sid.

"Bitter? Oh no. I understand the situation. I understood it then. I knew I had to go to school by listening to them talking. I heard my father say he didn't want me to go to an orphanage. I said, 'My goodness they're going to send me away.' So those ladies came and took me away in a car, took me straight there to my mother's house. I think it was in night-time when I got there."

I'm so tired.

We drive back to Sid and Pat's house. I don't want their time together to end. I want to provide one more opportunity for some sort of magic I expect to occur, so I invite the four to dinner, and I cannot believe I've done it.

Chapter 19

I rarely do such a thing for I do not consider myself to be a particularly good hostess, nor do I like to cook. Our house is often a disaster with children and dogs and cats passing in and out, piles of shoes at the door that none of my children remember to wear and stacks of newspaper clips on my desk that I've not organized yet. In spite of the chaos that occurs with four children, for me, the end of summer always seems bittersweet. I'll miss the hot nights catching frogs and debating Popsicle choices, finally learning which shade of the leftover yellows will be peach or coconut or banana. I always feel like I've left some summer fun undone, that the days slipped through my fingers like the mud my three boys—and daughter—coat themselves with on occasion.

But this year was the worst.

Kate, my youngest, started kindergarten. I know I should be happy. She's been counting the days since she finished preschool until she'd have the chance to walk the halls of the old elementary school. I ought to be glad she's been practicing her alphabet and assuring her brothers, "I'm going to like homework."

What a wonderful way to begin a life of learning.

But then she said, "Mom, you don't have to walk me in."

I knew I oughtn't to say it, but I did. "Kate, I want to walk you in."

This proved a dilemma for my five-year-old. On the one hand, she didn't want to hurt my feelings. On the other hand, she really did want to walk in to school all by herself.

A few days before her first day, she climbed into my lap.

"Mom, I have an idea," she announced. "We'll make a pattern. One day you can walk me in, the next day I'll walk in by myself. But I want the first day to be by myself. How does that sound?"

By this time I'd straightened out the proper mother role in my mind and knew what I needed to say.

"Kate, if you want to walk in by yourself, that's fine," I said. "I'm glad you're excited about school."

"I don't want to cramp your style," I joked, more for my benefit that hers.

Because then she added, "You can walk me in sometimes, Mom, but the first day I want to go in by myself. I just want to see what it feels like."

She's gone into that school—and even the same room with the same teacher—with every one of her three brothers. The teacher has talked to her since, well, since she could talk, and she's given her treats most visits, too. Kate clearly knew the routine, and she wanted to make it hers.

We all shopped for new clothes, new book bags and lunchboxes and notebooks and pencils and pencil boxes and crayons and paper and paper towels and magic soap. We loaded the book bags a week ahead of the start date, just to be sure we'd be ready.

Kate and I walked out to feed our goats and chickens the evening before she'd find out her teacher. "I hope I get Mrs. Hunt," she said. "I have to get Mrs. Hunt. I don't know any of the other teachers."

I didn't tell her that that's what I worry about as a parent, the uncertainty in a world where things have the potential to be so good, the little twist that can trigger a sadness, a fear, a hurt.

I took Kate, and I took my camera. I have photos of her grinning over her shoulder as she drags her massive rolling book bag—that I hand-painted—into the school. She casually strutted down the sidewalk with her hair finally brushed, her khaki skort swishing.

She let me walk with her through the first set of doors, and then we got to the brick courtyard.

"Mom, you can stop here," she said, then kissed me, hugged me and turned and continued alone into kindergarten.

I think of Mildred, and I think of her mother, and I think I can imagine how she felt. I know she loved her daughter. I believe she sent her daughter away to keep her safe.

Sid almost didn't come. I'd been surprised at his hesitation, for I'd invited his grandchildren to join us, and we had our own personal petting zoo to share with them. In the end, he came, but he didn't talk much. Before dinner, a light rain passed through, quickly clearing out as I showed Sid's grandchildren the goats. In the dusk sky above our home, a double rainbow formed. This is true. I took a picture of Mildred and Bill beneath it. I'd wanted Sid to stand with Mildred below the colors, but he didn't leave the air conditioning.

We've shared a simple dinner of hamburgers, coleslaw and chocolate chess pie. Our spouses have chatted; we've talked about growing up, about goats, about children and grandchildren.

"This coleslaw is really good," Sid tells me. He knows I don't like to cook.

"It certainly is," Mildred echoes, and I confess that I've left out half the ingredients.

"I like it just the way it is," Sid says.

The evening needs to end. We begin our goodbyes.

Sid hugs Mildred.

"Love you," says Sid. Tall, too skinny.

"Love you, too, Sid." Mildred's manicured nails show bright pink against his worn blue chambray shirt.

I feel like I'm eavesdropping on the pair, but they're standing in my house.

I just can't make myself look away when I see Sid hug Mildred. I know I need to remember this evening, and I file it away as a scene in my subconscious to visit when I miss him.

Epilogue

I waited, you know, for my maypops to bloom this summer. I watched my roses brown as vines climbed over them. One morning, I noticed the flowers. Blue morning glories. They weren't a sign from Sid after all. I'd mistaken the vine and its symbolism from the start, much like I'd mistaken the purpose of my time with Sid. I'm writing the story now using the gift of the memory he gave me, trusting his faith in me, remembering his words, "You can do this."

I may have been his last project, and I know he left me a tremendous legacy.

I drive to Stem, and I pass the little country church where I've been told Mildred's father may lie. I pray he's there. It brings me comfort. I stop and check his graveside occasionally to see if there are any new flowers beside his stone. For years I worried that he may have been killed because of his love for Mildred's mother, but I see his name, the date, and I trust he survived. I'm choosing to leave it at that.

I knew from the first time I met Sid that I wanted to write his story, and I felt from the first that I was meant to. What I didn't know is what I would learn because of him.

It wasn't until the end of this project that I figured out that it really wasn't for Sid that I was meant to write this after all. It's like he told me, though. He'd almost always start with a photograph when he painted, but once he got halfway through a painting, it dictated what it became. As I finish researching, interviewing and writing for nearly three years without Sid here, I've struggled with what to do, prayed about what to write.

I know now that in the end, I was meant to complete what he tried to do.

Sid wanted to reunite a family. But the discomfort and shame was too deep among the remaining family members he contacted to confront each other, and he respected that.

He believed all along that Mildred's white family loved her. I've felt love throughout this story. I suspect it's the love that had haunted Sid since he'd seen the tiny child sent away. He was right all along. They loved her. That I know.

As I continued down my list of people to call after Sid died, almost 18 months later I finally reached Rick Hensley, a Virginia potter. When I explained why I was calling, he became very quiet. And then I understood why.

"Do people still cry when they talk about him?" he asked.

They didn't really even like each other at first. In later years, though, Sid saw Hensley at a show unloading a kiln of his work. He walked right up and said, "I'm going to buy this pot."

The piece was a large, highly detailed blue and white porcelain bowl. Sid bought it and put it in his Museum of American Pottery. Later, Hensley spent almost a decade away from potting, but he started back again in the 1990's. Sid took him in the little museum room and said, "Here, I want you to have this back." He knew before Hensley did how important the piece would be to the young man.

After Sid died, I talked with Joe Osborne, who was a long-haired hippie-type, guitar-playing 13-year-old when he met Sid on a shopping trip with his mother in the 1980's.

"So do you play?" Sid asked.

"Guitar, acoustic and electric." Osborne tried to act cool.

"Why don't you bring your acoustic out and play at next week's kiln opening?" Sid said.

The teen's mother drove him to the gallery. It was the first gig for which he'd ever been paid more than $2, after his makeshift band split their fee. Sid sat the musician in a corner and gave him a little out of the drawer.

"It wasn't really about the money, but his encouragement, despite the fact that I wasn't really that good," Osborne said. "God puts us in the right place at the right time. Had I not experienced that one dose of encouragement…that was the moment that I said, 'I can do this, and this is what I do.'"

Perhaps Michael Sherrill said it best: "Although Sid's material was clay and paint, his real material was the human factor of interacting with people. He spent most of his time sitting in the chair drinking coffee."

Sid listened.

He gave me a beautiful pot. I learned he'd given away hundreds of pots. And I've learned that what he did for me—the listening, the encouraging—he did for hundreds of people.

Yet, even knowing what I know now, for some reason, I still trust his faith in me. I still believe he saw something in me. That was his biggest gift, I've decided, even if he did that for most everyone he encountered. He believed in people.

He did that for Mildred, too.

In one of our conversations, she spoke of when Sid called her the first time. "He told me he remembered what I had on all those any years ago. He remembered me sitting in the hallway by myself. He knew it was wrong."

In finding Mildred, I learned that, as she said, "You can't walk in someone else's shoes." I learned that it's not my place to judge people who lived in a time I can't begin to fathom. I learned about all sorts of layers of love.

And though all my life I'd been taught not to spread rumors, I know now that I would have never found her if I hadn't named her.

When Mildred and Bill visited, that's when I realized just how hard it was for Sid to breathe. I'd noticed myself talking more on the tapes of his interviews, and I'd chastised myself for interrupting or filling in silences when I could have captured more of his thoughts. It was only later that I figured out I was talking more because he was talking less.

One of the last times we spoke, he said to me, "I just want you to know I always look forward to talking with you. Some people I just talk to because I have to, but it was never like that with you. I mean that."

I know he knew me, knew I'd worry, knew I'd doubt myself.

Mildred brought her oldest daughter and three grandchildren down to Cedar Creek. She wanted them to meet the man who had never forgotten her. He began using an inhaler and oxygen as Mildred suggested, and I believe that gave him more time in the end.

Sid died just five months after we found Mildred.

Through our journey I saw that everyone edits his own life, that everyone decides how to be to whom. I know now that he probably tried to control me a little in the end, or maybe even a lot, though I don't think he'd like to think that he was doing that.

I wish Mildred and Sid could have grown up together. I bet they would have been friends. He was drawn to feisty women who spoke their minds. But if Mildred had grown up with her white family, she would have been a different person after all.

I've called her every few months to update her on my writing. After her visit, Mildred stayed at home almost all the time, tied to the oxygen that fills her lungs, suffering from emphysema that killed Sid.

"You call back any time, baby," she'd tell me. She died this spring.

I'm still amazed she ever talked to me. She trusted me the first time I called her. Finding Mildred taught me about grace and strength, about forgiveness and faith.

I've been unable to write about Sid in the past tense. I've kept myself busy with his story, avoiding the grief I know will come when I realize that he truly isn't here any longer.

I still look for signs from him. In a gift basket we received, I found chocolate covered coffee beans, fancy graham crackers, bottled water. An RC Cola. This time I write a note on it and tape it to the bottle in the refrigerator. "Do not drink this. Mom's." It must have come from him.

I almost cried once, just after I spoke at his funeral in 2004, but I stopped myself because I knew I had more to do to finish our project together.

Now I can cry.

From Tally-Ho to Stem, NC by Ethel O. Blalock, Town Historian, August 31, 1999.

Going Back Home by Ethel Oakley Blalock, 1999.

Richard H. Thornton Library in Granville County.

"Historical Narrative of Our Past," by Elizabeth Strater Marrow in *Shaw High Memories Back to Our Roots Third Grand Reunion June 17-19, 2005.*

Roaming Around Northern Granville County and Vicinity Places—People--Facts by John H. Wilson, Jr.

The Grandurson Story: A Narrative of War and the People by Ben M. Patrick, September 1945, Atlanta, Ga.

The Present Day Ku Klux Klan Movement Report by the Committee on Un-American Activities House of Representatives, Ninetieth Congress First Session released Dec. 11, 1967.

Printed in the United States
93268LV00004B/110/A